영어 리딩 학습의 최종 목표는 독해력 향상에 있습니다.

학년이 올라갈수록 영어 시험 출제가 늘어나는 논픽션 리딩을 통해 다양한 분야의 어휘와 지식을 습득하고 문제 해결 능력을 키울 수 있습니다. 또한 생활 속 실용문과 시험 상황의 복잡한 지문을 이해하고 분석하며, 나에게 필요한 정보를 추출하는 연습을 할 수 있습니다. 논픽션 독해력은 비판적 사고와 논리적 사고를 발전시키고, 영어로 표현된 아이디어를 깊이 있게 이해하고 효과적으로 소통하는 언어 능력을 갖출 수 있도록 도와줍니다.

미국교과서는 논픽션 리딩에 가장 적합한 학습 도구입니다.

미국교과서는 과학, 사회과학, 역사, 예술, 문학 등 다양한 주제의 폭넓은 지식과 이해를 제공하며, 사실을 그대로 받아들이는 능력뿐만 아니라 텍스트 너머의 맥락에 대한 비판적 사고와 분석 능력도 함께 배울 수 있도록 구성되어 있습니다. 미국 교과과정 주제의 리딩을 통해 학생들은 현실적인 주제를 탐구하고, 아카데믹한 어휘를 학습하면서 논리적 탐구의 방법을 함께 배울 수 있습니다. 미국교과서는 논픽션 독해력 향상을 위한 최고의 텍스트입니다.

탁월한 논픽션 독해력을 원한다면
미국교과서 READING 시리즈

(1) 미국교과서의 핵심 주제들을 엄선하여 담은 지문을 읽으며 **독해력**이 향상되고 **배경지식**이 쌓입니다.

(2) 가지고 있는 지식과 새로운 정보를 연결해 내 것으로 만드는 **통합사고력**을 기를 수 있습니다.

(3) 꼼꼼히 읽고 완전히 소화할 수 있도록 하는 수준별 독해 훈련으로 **문제 해결력**이 향상됩니다.

(4) 기초 문장 독해에서 추론까지, 학습자의 **수준별로 선택하여 학습**할 수 있도록 난이도를 설계하였습니다.

(5) 스스로 계획하고 점검하며 실력을 쌓아가는 **자기주도력**이 형성됩니다.

Author Suejeong Shin

She has been an adjunct professor of English Education at Yonsei University since 2017. Her research centers around the implementation of cognitive psychology to foster literacy development among young English language learners in Korea. In addition to her role in the classroom, she demonstrates visionary leadership as the founder of We Read, a literacy company.

With an impressive collection of sixty children's picture book titles and over 200 literacy-focused textbooks, she is an accomplished author and an expert in her field. She actively engages in the development of an innovative literacy curation service, ensuring that children have positive reading experiences in English. Equipped with a Ph.D. in cognitive science from Yonsei University, Suejeong's transformative work can be further explored on her captivating website at www.drsue.co.kr.

미국교과서 READING LEVEL 2 ❷
American Textbook Reading *Second Edition*

Second Published on August 14, 2023
Second Printed on August 30, 2023

First Published on November 27, 2015

Written by Suejeong Shin
Researcher Dain Song
Editorial Manager Namhui Kim, Seulgi Han
Design Kichun Jang, Hyeonsook Lee
Development Editor Mina Park
Proofreading Ryan P. Lagace, Benjamin Schultz
Typesetting Yeon Design
Illustrations Eunhyung Ryu, Hyoju Kim, Jongeun Yang
Recording Studio YR Media
Photo Credit shutterstock.com

Published and distributed by Gilbutschool

56, Worldcup-ro 10-gil, Mapo-gu, Seoul, Korea, 121-842
Tel 02-332-0931
Fax 02-322-0586
Homepage www.gilbutschool.co.kr
Publisher Jongwon Lee

ISBN   979-11-6406-542-4 (64740)
        979-11-6406-536-3 (set)
(Gilbutschool code : 30540)

미국교과서 리딩

READING

LEVEL 2 ②

길벗스쿨

LEVEL 2 논픽션 리딩 시작

1 미국 교과과정 주제의 픽션(50%)과 논픽션(50%) 지문을 고루 읽으며 균형 있는 읽기 실력을 키웁니다.

학생들의 인지 수준과 흥미를 반영한 다양한 토픽으로 하나의 주제 아래 Fiction과 Nonfiction 지문을 고루 읽을 수 있습니다. 이와 같은 반복적인 접근을 통하여 교과 주제에 더욱 익숙해지고 생각의 폭을 넓힐 수 있습니다.

2 기초 논픽션 주제 어휘와 패턴 문형을 중심으로 다양한 형식의 글을 학습합니다.

본격 논픽션 리딩 학습을 시작하기 전, 반복되는 패턴 문형 안에서 낯선 논픽션 어휘에 적응할 수 있도록 합니다. 또한 스토리 형식이나 설명문과 더불어 메뉴판, 편지글, 안내문 등 다양한 문형을 통하여 실용적인 텍스트를 이해하는 기초를 다집니다.

3 간단한 문장 구조의 글을 읽고, 다양한 문제를 경험하며 독해의 기본기를 튼튼하게 합니다.

지문을 읽고 핵심 주제, 세부 내용, 감정 표현, 문장 완성하기 등 다양한 문제를 통하여 읽은 내용을 파악합니다. 선택지에서 지문과 일치하는 부분을 찾아 단순히 답을 고르기 보다는 한번 더 생각하고 문제를 해결할 수 있도록 구성하여 독해의 기본기를 다집니다.

4 도표를 활용한 전체 내용 통합 활동으로 기초 리딩 스킬을 연습합니다.

도표 활동은 글의 구조를 확인하는 것과 동시에 어휘를 활용하는 능력에도 큰 도움이 됩니다. 길지 않은 지문이지만, 세부적인 내용을 확인한 이후 전체적으로 내용을 통합하고 정리하는 활동을 통하여 리딩 스킬을 익힐 수 있습니다.

Week 1

UNIT 01
Student Book ☐
Workbook ☐
DATE

UNIT 02
Student Book ☐
Workbook ☐

UNIT 03
Student Book ☐
Workbook ☐

UNIT 04
Student Book ☐
Workbook ☐

Week 2

UNIT 05
Student Book ☐
Workbook ☐
DATE

UNIT 06
Student Book ☐
Workbook ☐

UNIT 07
Student Book ☐
Workbook ☐

UNIT 08
Student Book ☐
Workbook ☐

Week 3

UNIT 09
Student Book ☐
Workbook ☐
DATE

UNIT 10
Student Book ☐
Workbook ☐

UNIT 11
Student Book ☐
Workbook ☐

UNIT 12
Student Book ☐
Workbook ☐

Week 4

UNIT 13
Student Book ☐
Workbook ☐
DATE

UNIT 14
Student Book ☐
Workbook ☐

UNIT 15
Student Book ☐
Workbook ☐

UNIT 16
Student Book ☐
Workbook ☐

Week 5

UNIT 17
Student Book ☐
Workbook ☐
DATE

UNIT 18
Student Book ☐
Workbook ☐

UNIT 19
Student Book ☐
Workbook ☐

UNIT 20
Student Book ☐
Workbook ☐

Before Reading

배경지식을 묻는 질문에 답하고,
주제별 어휘를 익히며 글의 내용을 예측해 봅니다.

QR코드를 스캔하여
정확한 발음 확인하기

Talk About It

경험을 묻는 질문에 답하며
주제를 대략적으로 파악해
보고, 배경지식을 활성화
합니다.

Words to Know

단어를 듣고 따라 말하며
익히고, 그림을 통해 뜻을
유추합니다.

Reading

미국교과서 핵심 주제의 픽션, 논픽션 글을 읽으며
교과 지식과 독해력을 쌓습니다.

Reading Passage

제목과 그림을 통해 내용을
먼저 예측해 봅니다.
음원을 들으면서 글을 읽고,
중심 내용과 세부 내용을
파악합니다.

Key Expressions

글에 사용된 패턴 문형
대화를 듣고 따라 말하며
익힙니다.

After Reading

다양한 유형의 문제를 풀며 읽은 내용을 확인하고,
단어와 문장을 점검합니다.

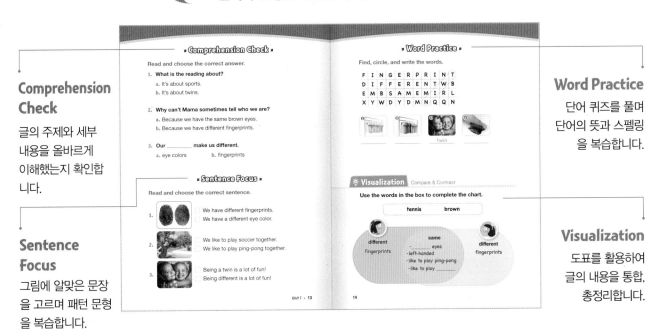

Comprehension Check

글의 주제와 세부 내용을 올바르게 이해했는지 확인합니다.

Sentence Focus

그림에 알맞은 문장을 고르며 패턴 문형을 복습합니다.

Word Practice

단어 퀴즈를 풀며 단어의 뜻과 스펠링을 복습합니다.

Visualization

도표를 활용하여 글의 내용을 통합, 총정리합니다.

Workbook

핵심 어휘와 주요 문장을 복습합니다.

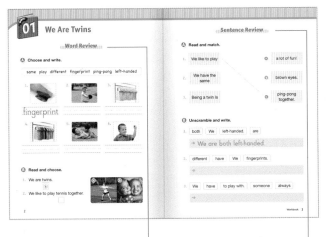

Word Review

이미지를 활용하여 단어의 의미를 복습합니다.

Sentence Review

문장 완성하기, 순서 배열하기 활동으로 패턴 문형과 어순을 복습합니다.

무료 온라인 학습 자료

길벗스쿨 e클래스

(eclass.gilbut.co.kr)에 접속하시면 〈미국교과서 READING〉 시리즈에 대한 상세 정보 및 부가학습 자료를 무료로 이용하실 수 있습니다.

1. 음원 스트리밍 및 MP3 파일
2. 추가 워크시트 4종
   단어 테스트, 문장 따라 쓰기, 해석 테스트, 리딩 지문 테스트
3. 복습용 온라인 퀴즈

★ 목차 ★

We Are Twins

Talk About It 🎧

1. Look at the twins in the picture. How are they alike?
2. How are they different?

▪ Words to Know ▪

Listen and repeat. 🎧

twin

same

left-handed

play

ping-pong

tennis

different

fingerprint

We Are Twins 🎧

We are twins.

We have the same brown eyes.
We are both left-handed.
Sometimes, Mama can't tell who we are!

Being a twin is a lot of fun!
We always have someone to play with.
We like to play ping-pong together.
We like to play tennis together.

There is one thing that makes us different.
We have different fingerprints.
Can you tell the difference?

Key Expressions

A : How are you alike?
B : We have the same blue eyes.

▪ Comprehension Check ▪

Read and choose the correct answer.

1. What is the reading about?

    a. It's about sports.

    b. It's about twins.

2. Why can't Mama sometimes tell who we are?

    a. Because we have the same brown eyes.

    b. Because we have different fingerprints.

3. Our _____ make us different.

    a. eye colors   **b.** fingerprints

▪ Sentence Focus ▪

Read and choose the correct sentence.

1.

☐ We have different fingerprints.
☐ We have a different eye color.

2.

☐ We like to play soccer together.
☐ We like to play ping-pong together.

3.

☐ Being a twin is a lot of fun!
☐ Being different is a lot of fun!

▪ Word Practice ▪

Find, circle, and write the words.

F	I	N	G	E	R	P	R	I	N	T
D	I	F	F	E	R	E	N	T	W	B
E	M	B	S	A	M	E	M	I	R	L
X	Y	W	D	Y	D	M	N	Q	Q	N

_____

_____

twin

_____

☀ Visualization   Compare & Contrast

Use the words in the box to complete the chart.

tennis   brown

different

fingerprints

same

· _____ eyes
· left-handed
· like to play ping-pong
· like to play _____

different

fingerprints

14

Fingerprints

Talk About It 🎧

1 What is the person doing in the picture?
2 Why are fingerprints so important?

▪ Words to Know ▪

Listen and repeat. 🎧

pencil

scribble

paper

rub

thumb

tape

put

press

Fingerprints 🎧

What do your fingerprints look like?

No two fingerprints are exactly the same.
But most people's fingerprints look like these.

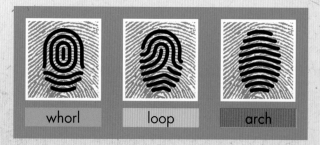

whorl   loop   arch

Take a pencil and scribble on a piece of paper.
Then, rub your thumb.
Now, get some tape.
Put a piece of tape over your thumb,
press down, and pull it off.
Then, put the tape on a piece of paper.

What does your thumbprint
look like?

💬 **Key Expressions**

A : What does your thumbprint
look like?
B : It looks like a whorl.

Comprehension Check

Read and choose the correct answer.

1. What is the reading about?

   a. It's about fingerprints.

   b. It's about the thumb.

2. What should you do before you get some tape?

   a. I should rub my thumb on the paper.

   b. I should put a piece of tape over my thumb.

3. No two _____ are exactly the same.

   a. tapes   b. fingerprints

Sentence Focus

Read and choose the correct sentence.

1.
   ☐ Some people's fingerprints look like whorls.
   ☐ Some people's fingerprints look like loops.

2.
   ☐ Take a piece of paper.
   ☐ Scribble on a piece of paper.

3.
   ☐ Put the tape over your thumb.
   ☐ Put the tape on a piece of paper.

▪ Word Practice ▪

Find, circle, and write the words.

P	M	J	T	B	J	T
E	J	N	R	P	H	R
N	Z	N	Y	U	U	P
C	Z	L	M	B	Y	T
I	X	B	D	J	Z	R
L	T	W	N	B	N	Z

①

②

③

put

④

_____   _____   _____   _____

💡 Visualization Main Idea & Details

Use the words in the box to complete the chart.

Fingerprints   tape

Main Idea

_____

Detail

No two fingerprints are exactly the same.

Detail

Most people's fingerprints look like whorls, loops, or arches.

Detail

You need a pencil, _____ and paper to print your fingerprints.

18

A Perfect Shell

Talk About It

1 What do you know about hermit crabs?
2 What does a hermit crab carry on its back?

▪ Words to Know ▪

Listen and repeat.

move

shell

perfect

heavy

fancy

plain

find

just right

A Perfect Shell 🎧

It's time to move.
I've grown too big for
my little shell.

Is this the perfect shell?
No, this shell is too big for me.

Is this the perfect shell?
No, this shell is too heavy for me.

Is this the perfect shell?
No, this shell is too fancy for me.

Is this the perfect shell?
No, this shell is too plain for me.

I've found the perfect shell!
A shell that is just right for me.

💬 **Key Expressions**

A : Is this the perfect shell?
B : No, this shell is too big
    for me.

20

▲ hermit crab

▪ Comprehension Check ▪

Read and choose the correct answer.

1. **Who am I?**

   a. I'm a shell.

   b. I'm a hermit crab.

2. **Why do I need to move?**

   a. Because I've grown too big.

   b. Because my shell is too heavy.

3. **I am looking for the _____ shell.**

   a. big   b. perfect

▪ Sentence Focus ▪

Read and choose the correct sentence.

1.

   ☐ This shell is too heavy for me.

   ☐ This shell is too little for me.

2.

   ☐ This shell is too fancy for me.

   ☐ This shell is too plain for me.

3.

   ☐ I've found the heavy shell!

   ☐ I've found the perfect shell!

◾ Word Practice ◾

Find, circle, and write the words.

J	U	S	T	R	I	G	H	T
F	X	H	R	S	T	J	T	D
I	L	P	E	M	H	Q	R	P
N	J	J	M	A	D	E	B	L
D	W	Z	N	L	V	X	L	K
X	X	Y	M	V	R	Y	M	L

①_____   ② __heavy__   ③_____   ④_____

☼ Visualization   Cause & Effect

Use the words in the box to complete the chart.

> perfect   move

Why?

I've grown too big for my little shell.

What Happened?

It's time to _____.

Why?

This shell is just right for me.

What Happened?

This is the _____ shell.

Homes Around the World

Talk About It 🎧

1 Where do you live?
2 How does your house help you to live?

▪ Words to Know ▪

Listen and repeat. 🎧

home

houseboat

family

catch

underground house

cool

heat

safe

Homes Around the World 🎧

Homes are different around the world.

Rudee lives in Thailand.
She lives in a houseboat.
It helps her family to catch fish for a living.

▲ houseboat

Aziz lives in Tunisia.
He lives in an underground house.
It helps his family to keep cool from the heat.

Mongo lives in Mongolia.
She lives in a yurt.
It helps her family to go everywhere they want.

▼ underground house

Alaa lives in a refugee camp.
He lives in a tent.
It helps his family to live safe.

▼ yurt

Key Expressions
A : Where do you live?
B : I live in a houseboat.

24

Comprehension Check

Read and choose the correct answer.

1. What is the reading about?

   a. It's about homes.

   b. It's about the world.

2. How does a yurt help Mongo's family?

   a. It helps them to live safe.

   b. It helps them to go everywhere they want.

3. People live in different types of _____ .

   a. homes   b. tents

Sentence Focus

Read and choose the correct sentence.

1. ☐ She lives in an underground house.
   ☐ She lives in a yurt.

2. ☐ It helps her family to catch fish for a living.
   ☐ It helps her family to keep cool from the heat.

3. ☐ Alaa lives in a houseboat.
   ☐ Alaa lives in a refugee camp.

▪ Word Practice ▪

Find, circle, and write the words.

F	C	A	T	C	H	B
Q	A	Q	S	E	W	T
H	M	M	M	A	L	T
O	Y	O	I	Y	F	V
M	L	W	W	L	D	E
E	B	Z	T	Y	Y	J

safe

_____   _____   _____

☼ Visualization   Main Idea & Details

Use the words in the box to complete the chart.

> tent   houseboat

Homes are different around the world.

Thailand	Tunisia	Mongolia	Refugee Camp
_____	underground house	yurt	_____

Home Alone

Talk About It 🎧

1 Have you ever been home alone?

2 How do you like to be home alone?

• Words to Know •

Listen and repeat. 🎧

alone

busy

clean

messy

pretend

dragon

bored

turn

Home Alone 🎧

I am home alone.
All of my friends are busy.

I clean my messy room.
I make bubbles with shampoo.
I read my favorite book.
I pretend there's a dragon.
I watch TV with my eyes closed.
I'm still bored!

How can I turn my day into
a day of fun?
I can't think of a single fun thing to do.
What a boring day!

Key Expressions

A : What are you doing?
B : I am cleaning my messy room.

▪ Comprehension Check ▪

Read and choose the correct answer.

1. **Why am I home alone?**

   a. Because I have many things to do.

   b. Because all of my friends are busy.

2. **What is my problem?**

   a. I'm bored.

   b. I'm sick.

3. **I want to _____ my day into a fun day.**

   a. think   b. turn

▪ Sentence Focus ▪

Read and choose the correct sentence.

1.
   ☐ I am home alone.
   ☐ I am home with my friends.

2.
   ☐ I clean my messy room.
   ☐ I read my favorite book.

3.
   ☐ What a busy day!
   ☐ What a boring day!

▪ Word Practice ▪

Find, circle, and write the words.

C	A	L	O	N	E	T
L	M	E	S	S	Y	B
E	V	R	M	A	U	M
A	L	J	D	S	L	M
N	Q	P	Y	M	Z	Y

_____

busy

_____

_____

Visualization Problem & Solution

Use the words in the box to complete the chart.

bored   pretend

Problem	Solution

I _____ there's a dragon.

I am _____ .

I make bubbles with shampoo.

30

Big Game

Talk About It 🎧

1 What's your favorite sport?
2 Why do you like it?

▪ Words to Know ▪

Listen and repeat. 🎧

beat

kick

over

miss

upset

win

lose

coach

Big Game 🎧

Today is the big game.
We'll beat the Lion Team today.

We ran and kicked the ball.
The game was almost over.
I kicked the ball really hard.
But my shot missed the net.
I kicked it too high.
The Lion Team won the game.
I was very upset.

"It doesn't matter who wins or loses,"
said the coach.
"Yes, Jack! We tried our best!"
cried the Tiger Team happily.

Key Expressions
A : What did you do today?
B : I ran and kicked the ball.

▪ Comprehension Check ▪

Read and choose the correct answer.

1. What is the reading about?

    a. It's about the big game.

    b. It's about the Lion Team.

2. Why was I very upset?

    a. Because the Lion Team won the game.

    b. Because we beat the Lion Team.

3. In the picture, children are playing _____ .

    a. basketball   **b.** soccer

▪ Sentence Focus ▪

Read and choose the correct sentence.

1.
   ☐ We'll lose the game today.
   ☐ We'll win the game today.

2.
   ☐ I kicked the ball really hard.
   ☐ My shot missed the net.

3.
   ☐ I was very upset.
   ☐ We tried our best.

▪ Word Practice ▪

Find, circle, and write the words.

L	Z	W	K	C	U	M
L	I	A	O	I	O	I
N	O	A	E	W	C	S
J	C	S	Z	B	H	K
H	J	M	E	B	A	S

_____

win

_____

_____

☼ Visualization | Story Elements

Use the words in the box to complete the chart.

> missed   upset

Big Game

Who?		Feel How?		Why?
I	✛	very _____	✛	My shot _____ the net. The Lion Team won the game.
Tiger Team and I	✛	happy	✛	We did our best.

34

UNIT 07

Language Arts

Achoo!

Talk About It 🎧

1 How do you feel when you catch a cold?
2 What do you do when you catch a cold?

• Words to Know •

Listen and repeat. 🎧

shiver

ache

weak

put on

sweater

muffler

grandma

cold

Achoo!

I shiver.
My body aches.
I feel so weak. Achoo!

I put on my hat.
I put on my sweater.
I put on my muffler.
And I wrap myself in a blanket.

Grandma comes and says,
"This will help you, my dear."
I cry, "Oh, chicken soup!"

Hurray!
Now, I will not be cold anymore.
Grandma's chicken soup is always good.

💬 **Key Expressions**

A : How do you feel when
    you catch a cold?
B : I feel cold.

▪ Comprehension Check ▪

Read and choose the correct answer.

1. What's wrong with me?

  a. I shiver and my body aches.

  b. I wrap myself in a blanket.

2. What does Grandma do for me?

  a. She helps me put on my sweater.

  b. She makes chicken soup for me.

3. I like _____ .

  a. my blanket   b. Grandma's chicken soup

▪ Sentence Focus ▪

Read and choose the correct sentence.

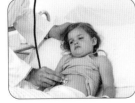

1.
☐ I feel so good.
☐ I feel so weak.

2.
☐ I put on my hat.
☐ I put on my muffler.

3.
☐ Grandma's sweater is good.
☐ Grandma's chicken soup is good.

▪ Word Practice ▪

Find, circle, and write the words.

S	W	E	A	T	E	R
A	W	P	U	T	O	N
C	E	E	Z	D	W	B
H	N	A	A	K	V	L
E	X	N	K	K	J	M

① weak

② _____

③ _____

④ _____

⚙ Visualization   Cause & Effect

Use the words in the box to complete the chart.

> Grandma   shiver

Why?		What Happened?
I _____.	⇒	I wrap myself in a blanket.
I eat _____'s chicken soup.	⇒	I will not be cold anymore.

Soups in Asia

Talk About It 🎧

1 How do you get over a cold?

2 Do you eat anything special for a cold?

Words to Know

Listen and repeat. 🎧

soup

get over

cold

Asia

potato

lizard

beef

feel better

Soups in Asia 🎧

People eat soup to get over a cold.
What kind of soup do people in Asia eat?

People in China eat potato soup for a cold.
People in Hong Kong eat lizard soup for a cold.
People in Japan eat miso soup for a cold.
People in Korea eat bean sprout soup for a cold.
People in Taiwan eat beef noodle soup for a cold.
People in Thailand eat chicken rice soup for a cold.

Soups differ around Asia.
But people eat soup to feel better in no time.

▼ potato soup

▼ miso soup

▼ beef noodle soup

💬 **Key Expressions**

A : What do you eat to get over a cold?
B : I eat chicken soup.

Comprehension Check

Read and choose the correct answer.

1. **What is the reading about?**

   a. It's about Asian soups for a cold.

   b. It's about Asians' favorite soup.

2. **What do people in Hong Kong eat for a cold?**

   a. They eat potato soup.

   b. They eat lizard soup.

3. **People eat different soups to get over _____.**

   a. a cold   b. the ache

Sentence Focus

Read and choose the correct sentence.

1.
   ☐ Soups differ around Asia.
   ☐ Noodles differ around Asia.

2.
   ☐ People in Taiwan eat beef noodle soup.
   ☐ People in China eat potato soup.

3.
   ☐ People eat soup to get over a cold.
   ☐ People eat bread to get over a cold.

▪ Word Practice ▪

Find, circle, and write the words.

F	E	E	L	B	E	T	T	E	R
P	O	T	A	T	O	J	T	S	J
Q	K	L	B	X	B	V	O	Z	W
Z	G	E	M	M	Y	U	M	P	D
D	E	Y	T	D	P	D	X	Q	B
F	B	M	J	L	N	Y	W	Y	W

_____   beef   _____   _____
          _____

💡 **Visualization**   Main Idea & Details

Use the words in the box to complete the chart.

> Asia   get over

Main Idea

Asian Soups for a Cold

Detail

People eat soup to _____ a cold.

Detail

Soups differ around _____ .

42

Why Do Elephants Have Trunks?

Talk About It 🎧

1. Look at the picture. How are they alike?
2. How are they different?

▪ Words to Know ▪

Listen and repeat. 🎧

wonder

lunch

river

ear

get close

bite

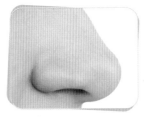

nose

trunk

Why Do Elephants Have Trunks? 🎧

Long ago, there was Little Elephant.

One morning, Little Elephant wondered,
"What does Mr. Crocodile eat for lunch?"
He went down the river to find the answer.

"Mr. Crocodile, what do you eat for lunch?"
"Come here, little one. I'll tell you in your ear."
Little Elephant got close to Mr. Crocodile.
Mr. Crocodile bit and pulled
Little Elephant's nose.
Little Elephant pulled his nose back.
Little Elephant was safe from Mr. Crocodile.

Since then, elephants have
had long trunks.

💬 **Key Expressions**
A : What did Little Elephant do?
B : He went down the river.

44

▪ Comprehension Check ▪

Read and choose the correct answer.

1. Who is the story about?

    a. It's about Mr. Crocodile.

    b. It's about Little Elephant.

2. Why did Little Elephant go down the river?

    a. to find out what Mr. Crocodile eats for lunch

    b. to find out what Mr. Crocodile does at lunch time

3. Mr. Crocodile bit Little Elephant's _____ .

    a. ear   **b.** nose

▪ Sentence Focus ▪

Read and choose the correct sentence.

1.
  ☐ He went down the river to eat lunch.
  ☐ He went down the river to meet Mr. Crocodile.

2.
  ☐ I'll tell you in your ear.
  ☐ I'll tell you in your nose.

3.
  ☐ An elephant has a short trunk.
  ☐ An elephant has a long trunk.

Word Practice

Find, circle, and write the words.

W	O	N	D	E	R	B	T
J	I	B	N	C	L	K	E
Y	L	V	O	Y	Z	B	
R	I	V	E	R	S	M	I
G	S	Q	R	R	Y	E	T
G	E	T	C	L	O	S	E

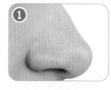

① nose

②

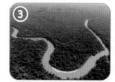

③

④

Visualization   Sequence

Use the words in the box to complete the chart. Then, number 1-4 to show the correct order.

bit   trunks

4

Elephants got long _____ .

"What does Mr. Crocodile eat for lunch?" Little Elephant wondered.

Mr. Crocodile _____ and pulled Little Elephant's nose.

"What do you eat for lunch?" Little Elephant asked.

46

Elephant Trunk

Talk About It 🎧

1 What do elephants do with their trunks?

2 How is your nose different from an elephant's trunk?

▪ Words to Know ▪

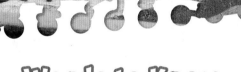

Listen and repeat. 🎧

breathe

smell

touch

spray

dust

body

pick up

protect

Elephant Trunk

Elephants have long trunks.
They breathe, smell, touch, eat,
and drink with their trunks.

This elephant can use its trunk
to dig for water.
This elephant can use its trunk
to spray dust over its body.
This elephant can use its trunk to drink water.
This elephant can use its trunk to pick up a peanut.
This elephant can use its trunk to touch its baby.
This elephant can use its trunk
to protect itself.

Elephants do many things
with their trunks.

Key Expressions

A : What can elephants do
with their trunks?
B : They can dig for water.

Comprehension Check

Read and choose the correct answer.

1. What is the reading about?

   a. It's about what elephants do with their trunks.

   b. It's about how elephants dig for water.

2. What do elephants do with their trunks?

   a. They can use their trunks to pick up a peanut.

   b. They can use their trunks to pick up a baby elephant.

3. Elephants _____, smell, touch, eat, and drink with their trunks.

   a. bite   **b.** breathe

Sentence Focus

Read and choose the correct sentence.

1.

  ☐ It can use its trunk to dig for water.

  ☐ It can use its trunk to spray water.

2.

  ☐ It can use its trunk to touch its baby.

  ☐ It can use its trunk to feed its baby.

3.

  ☐ It can use its trunk to drink water.

  ☐ It can use its trunk to protect itself.

• Word Practice •

Find, circle, and write the words.

P	R	O	T	E	C	T	S	B
S	I	R	M	O	G	L	P	O
R	M	C	I	T	U	Q	R	D
N	N	E	K	C	N	C	A	Y
M	B	U	L	U	K	P	H	E
J	C	T	T	L	P	Y	Y	H

① _____   ② _____   ③ touch   ④ _____

☀ Visualization Main Idea & Details

Use the words in the box to complete the chart.

> breathe   dust

Main Idea

Elephants do many things with their trunks.

Detail	Detail	Detail	Detail
Elephants can drink water with their trunks.	Elephants can spray _____ with their trunks.	Elephants can _____ with their trunks.	Elephants can eat with their trunks.

We're Not Afraid

Talk About It 🎧

1 Where do monsters live?

2 Are you afraid of monsters?

▪ Words to Know ▪

Listen and repeat. 🎧

afraid

library

gym

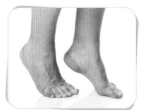

tiptoe

girl's room

boy's room

locker

shut

We're Not Afraid

We're going on a monster hunt.
We're not afraid!
Is the monster in the library?
Or is it in the gym?
Tiptoe, tiptoe.

We're going on a monster hunt.
We're not afraid!
Is the monster in the girl's room?
Or is it in the boy's room?
Tiptoe, tiptoe.

Aaahh!
There is a monster inside a locker!
Back to the boy's room,
back to the girl's room!
Back to the gym, back to the library!
Boom! Boom! Boom! Boom!
Shut the door! BANG!
We're not going on a monster
hunt again!

> **Key Expressions**
> A : Is the monster in the library?
> B : No.

Comprehension Check

Read and choose the correct answer.

1. What are we doing?

   a. We're going to school.

   b. We're going on a monster hunt.

2. Where do we find the monster?

   a. in the library

   b. inside a locker

3. We're _____ to go on a monster hunt again.

   a. afraid   b. not afraid

Sentence Focus

Read and choose the correct sentence.

1.
  ☐ Is the monster in the girl's room?
  ☐ Is the monster in the boy's room?

2.
  ☐ There is a monster inside a locker!
  ☐ There is a monster in the gym!

3.
  ☐ We go back to the gym.
  ☐ We go back to the library.

▪ Word Practice ▪

Find, circle, and write the words.

G	I	R	L	'	S	R	O	O	M	T
Z	M	U	Y	L	D	H	B	S	O	I
S	I	G	D	V	O	O	U	I	U	P
H	E	W	P	E	J	U	N	T	A	T
H	A	F	R	A	I	D	A	Y	U	O
R	F	B	L	E	V	M	T	P	J	E
E	B	E	D	K	H	A	J	F	C	N

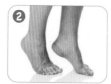

shut

_____   _____   _____   _____

💡 Visualization   Sequence

Use the words in the box to complete the chart. Then, number 1-5 to show the correct order of the places the kids visited in the story.

gym   library

_____

boy's room

girl's room

_____

locker

54

Field Trip

Talk About It 🎧

1 Have you ever been on a field trip?
2 Where did you go?

▪ Words to Know ▪

Listen and repeat. 🎧

field trip

aquarium

kid

starfish

tank

shark

dangerous

kill

Field Trip 🎧

April 8, 2023

Dear Diary,

Today, my class went on a field trip.
We went to the aquarium.
Every kid in the class came on the trip.

At the aquarium, we saw starfish in a tank.
We saw sharks swimming over our heads.
We saw box jellyfish.

I learned that box jellyfish are very dangerous.
They can kill a boy in three minutes!

We had a great day!
It was the best field trip we've had this year.

💬 **Key Expressions**

A : What did you see at the aquarium?
B : I saw box jellyfish.

Comprehension Check

Read and choose the correct answer.

1. **Where did my class go today?**

   a. My class went on a field trip to the aquarium.

   b. My class went on a field trip to the sea.

2. **What did we see at the aquarium?**

   a. We saw sharks swimming over our heads.

   b. We saw starfish attacking other fish.

3. **Box jellyfish are _____ because they can kill a boy.**

   a. dangerous   b. friendly

Sentence Focus

Read and choose the correct sentence.

1.

   ☐ My class went on a field trip.
   ☐ My class went fishing.

2.

   ☐ Every kid in the class came on the trip.
   ☐ No kids in the class came on the trip.

3.

   ☐ We saw starfish in a tank.
   ☐ We saw sharks in a tank.

▪ Word Practice ▪

Find, circle, and write the words.

D	A	N	G	E	R	O	U	S
F	I	E	L	D	T	R	I	P
M	Y	T	T	B	P	K	G	M
Q	K	I	L	L	Q	D	I	J
Z	D	I	O	G	D	X	J	D

_____ kid _____ _____

🔅 Visualization   Setting

Use the words in the box to complete the chart.

    sharks   tank   aquarium

Where?

the _____

What?

· We saw starfish in a _____.
· We saw _____ swimming over our heads.
· We saw dangerous box jellyfish.

UNIT 13 Ethics

No More Bullies!

Talk About It 🎧

1 How do you feel when your friend push you?
2 What can you say to the friend?

▪ Words to Know ▪

Listen and repeat. 🎧

shoulder

face

class photo

message

hurt

laugh

bully

nice

No More Bullies! 🎧

Francis pushed me on the shoulder.
"Don't," I said.

Jesse drew a big nose on my face
in the class photo.
"Don't," I said.

Stevie sent me the same message
for a week: "Nobody likes you!"
"Don't," I said.

I've fallen down in the gym and hurt myself.
The others laughed at me.

"Please, don't! No more bullies!
It hurts me very much.
That's not nice!" I cried.

💬 **Key Expressions**
A : Don't push me on the shoulder.
B : Sorry.

▪ Comprehension Check ▪

Read and choose the correct answer.

1. **What is the reading about?**

   a. It's about school bullying.

   b. It's about class photo.

2. **What can you tell about school bullying?**

   a. It is boring.

   b. It may hurt someone.

3. **I need to say _____ when someone bullies me.**

   a. "Don't."   **b.** "I'm sorry."

▪ Sentence Focus ▪

Read and choose the correct sentence.

1.
  ☐ He pushed me on the shoulder.
  ☐ He hit me on the head.

2.
  ☐ He laughed at me.
  ☐ He sent me a message.

3.
  ☐ "No more bullies!" I cried.
  ☐ "That's nice!" I cried.

▪ Word Practice ▪

Find, circle, and write the words.

S	H	O	U	L	D	E	R	L
N	K	F	J	B	V	B	A	Y
I	P	M	A	T	U	U	R	M
C	M	W	R	C	G	P	L	B
E	Y	Y	H	H	E	L	V	Y

_____   _____   __laugh___   _____

☀ Visualization   Cause & Effect

Use the words in the box to complete the chart.

    hurts   message

Why?		What Happened?
Francis pushed me on the shoulder.		
Jesse drew a big nose on my face in the class photo.	→	It _____ me very much.
Stevie sent me the same bad _____ for a week.		

62

Social Media Etiquette

Talk About It

1 Do you use social media?
2 How do you use social media?

▪ Words to Know ▪

Listen and repeat.

etiquette

chat

comments

social media

post

true

kind

tag

Social Media Etiquette

Do you like to chat on social media?
Do you like to write comments on social media?
Do you like to tag your friends on social media?

Think before you post on social media.
Think about if your message is true.
Think about if your comment is kind.
Think about if it is okay to tag your friends.

Remember that social media can be dangerous.
You may hurt your friends.

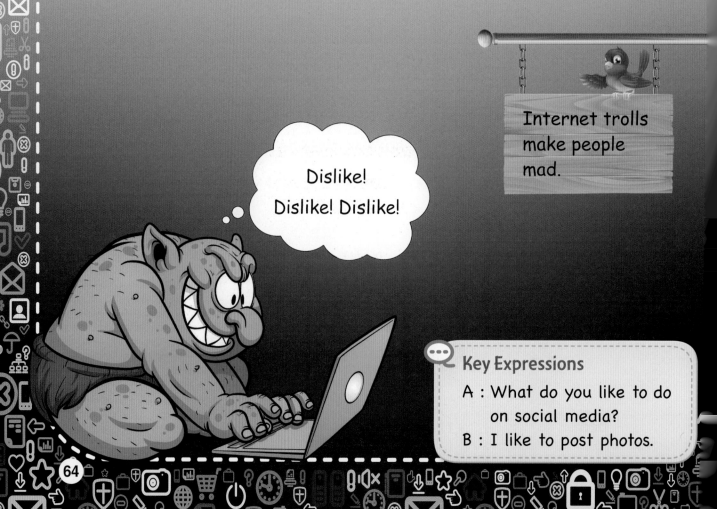

Internet trolls make people mad.

Dislike!
Dislike! Dislike!

Key Expressions

A : What do you like to do
on social media?
B : I like to post photos.

▪ Comprehension Check ▪

Read and choose the correct answer.

1. **What is the reading about?**

   a. It's about why social media etiquette is important.

   b. It's about how to write comments on social media.

2. **What should you do before you act on social media?**

   a. I should think about if the message is fun.

   b. I should think about if the message is true.

3. **Social media can be _____.**

   a. dangerous   **b.** helpful

▪ Sentence Focus ▪

Read and choose the correct sentence.

1.
   ☐ Do you like to chat on social media?
   ☐ Do you like to hurt your friends?

2.
   ☐ Think about if the message is fun.
   ☐ Think about if the message is kind.

3.
   ☐ Social media may hurt someone.
   ☐ Social media may help someone.

Word Practice

Find, circle, and write the words.

L	U	F	R	E	W	O	P
L	P	D	D	C	T	A	G
B	O	N	H	K	I	N	D
G	S	A	K	R	N	D	L
S	T	D	P	J	R	R	X

① _____ ② _____ ③ chat ④ _____

Visualization — Cause & Effect

Use the words in the box to complete the chart.

> Social media   true

Why?

The message is not _____.

The comment is not kind.

The message is not helpful.

What Happened?

_____ may hurt someone.

66

Animal Teeth

UNIT 15 Language Arts

Talk About It 🎧

1 What do children eat?
2 Can you describe what your teeth look like?

▪ Words to Know ▪

Listen and repeat. 🎧

tooth

flat

plant

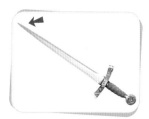

sharp

large

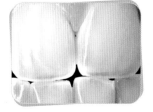

front teeth

chew

fight

Animal Teeth 🎧

Oh me oh my!
What flat teeth you have!
My flat teeth help me to eat plants.

Oh me oh my!
What sharp teeth you have!
My sharp teeth help me to eat animals.

Oh me oh my!
What large front teeth you have!
My large front teeth help me to chew branches.

Oh me oh my!
What enormous teeth you have!
My enormous teeth help me to fight.

I have flat and sharp teeth.
What do you think I eat?

▲ horse

▼ tiger

▲ beaver

▲ hippo

💬 **Key Expressions**

A : What flat teeth you have!
B : My flat teeth help me
    to eat plants.

Comprehension Check

Read and choose the correct answer.

1. **What is the reading about?**

   a. It's about animals' food.

   b. It's about animal teeth.

2. **How do animals use their teeth?**

   a. Some animals eat with their teeth.

   b. Some animals grab with their teeth.

3. **A horse's flat teeth help it to eat _____.**

   a. branches   b. plants

Sentence Focus

Read and choose the correct sentence.

1.

   ☐ What flat teeth you have!

   ☐ What sharp teeth you have!

2.

   ☐ I have tiny teeth.

   ☐ I have enormous teeth.

3.

   ☐ My teeth help me to chew branches.

   ☐ My teeth help me to fight.

· Word Practice ·

Find, circle, and write the words.

T	V	F	P	A	K	N	F
O	V	V	F	L	Y	F	I
O	Q	A	H	L	A	C	G
T	O	F	L	A	T	N	H
H	T	P	U	J	C	B	T

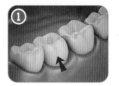 ①
 ②
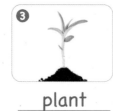 ③
 ④

_____   _____   __plant__   _____

Visualization   Categorize

Use the words in the box to complete the chart.

> chew   Sharp

Animal Teeth

Flat Teeth
· eat plants
· a horse

Large Front Teeth
· _____ branches
· a beaver

_____ Teeth
· eat animals
· a tiger

Enormous Teeth
· fight
· a hippo

UNIT 16 Science

Some Animals Lay Eggs

Talk About It 🎧

1 What animals come from eggs?

2 How do young animals break through the eggshell?

▪ Words to Know ▪

Listen and repeat. 🎧

lay an egg

color

young animal

grow

egg tooth

break

eggshell

hatch

Some Animals Lay Eggs 🎧

Some animals lay eggs.
Some animals lay just one egg at a time.
Other animals lay many eggs at once.

Eggs come in many different shapes.
Eggs come in many different sizes.
Eggs come in many different colors.

Young animals grow safely inside eggs.
Many young animals have an egg tooth.
The egg tooth helps the young animal
break through the eggshell.

The egg tooth falls off after the
young animal hatches.

💬 **Key Expressions**

A : What do you know about eggs?
B : Eggs come in many different
     sizes.

Comprehension Check

Read and choose the correct answer.

1. What is the reading about?

a. It's about young animals.

b. It's about animal eggs.

2. What helps many young animals break through the eggshell?

a. an egg tooth

b. adult animals

3. After a young animal _____, the egg tooth falls off.

a. hatches   b. grows

Sentence Focus

Read and choose the correct sentence.

1.
☐ Some animals lay just one egg at a time.
☐ Some animals lay many eggs at once.

2.
☐ Eggs come in many different colors.
☐ Eggs come in many different shapes.

3.
☐ Young animals grow safely inside eggs.
☐ Young animals break through the eggshell.

• Word Practice •

Find, circle, and write the words.

H	G	W	N	V	M	W	C
A	V	G	Y	N	O	Y	O
T	B	R	E	A	K	T	L
C	X	R	G	R	O	W	O
H	T	Y	B	T	A	Y	R
M	L	W	R	B	K	M	A

_____   grow   _____   _____

⚙ Visualization   Main Idea & Details

Use the words in the box to complete the chart.

> colors   egg tooth

Main Idea

Some animals lay eggs.

Detail

· just one egg at a time
· many eggs at once

Detail

· different shapes
· different sizes
· different _____

Detail

· grow safely inside eggs
· have an _____

74

UNIT 17

Language Arts

Night Walk

Talk About It 🎧

1 How often do you walk outside at night?

2 What do you see?

▪ Words to Know ▪

Listen and repeat. 🎧

window

moon

miss

night

street

dark

glow

arrive

Night Walk 🎧

I look out the window.
I see the moon.
It looks like Grandma's face.
"Dad, I miss Grandma.
Can I go and see her now?" I say.

Dad and I walk out in the night.
Grandma lives on the other side of the street.
It is dark outside.
It is hard to see things in the dark.
But it is easy to find a light in the dark.
"Look! Stars shine even brighter
today!" I cry.
We walk and see something
glowing in the dark.
"Meow!"
It is Kitty, Grandma's cat.
We have already arrived at
Grandma's house.

Key Expressions
A : What do you see in
the night sky?
B : I see stars in the
night sky.

76

▪ Comprehension Check ▪

Read and choose the correct answer.

1. **What do I see outside the window?**

    a. I see Grandma's face.

    b. I see the moon.

2. **Where do Dad and I go?**

    a. to Grandma's house

    b. to the park

3. **It is easy to find _____ in the dark.**

    a. Grandma's house   **b.** a light

▪ Sentence Focus ▪

Read and choose the correct sentence.

1.
☐ I see Grandma's cat.
☐ I see the moon.

2.
☐ We arrived at Grandma's house.
☐ We walked out to Grandma's house.

3.
☐ We see something glowing in the dark.
☐ We see something flying in the dark.

▪ Word Practice ▪

Find, circle, and write the words.

S	W	I	N	D	O	W	A
W	T	Y	N	K	Q	R	B
N	N	R	J	I	R	X	V
B	W	Z	E	I	G	T	T
R	J	Q	V	E	M	H	Y
M	P	E	P	Y	T	R	T

arrive

_____   _____   _____   _____

☀ Visualization   Cause & Effect

Use the words in the box to complete the chart.

> dark   miss

Why?		**What Happened?**
I _____ Grandma.		Dad and I go to see Grandma.
It is easy to find a light in the _____ .		We see Kitty's eyes glowing in the dark.

78

Star Jar

Talk About It

1 Do you like to watch the stars?

2 When can you watch the stars?

• Words to Know •

Listen and repeat.

jar

tinfoil

roll

paper clip

poke

wrap

turn on

turn off

Star Jar 🎧

Let's make a star jar.

Material
jar, tinfoil, scissors, paper clip, tape, smartphone

Measure the Tinfoil

1. Take a jar and roll tinfoil around it.
2. Cut the tinfoil.

Make Stars

3. Use a paper clip to poke holes in the tinfoil.
4. Poke as many holes as you want.

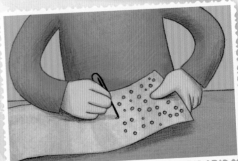

Star Jar

5. Wrap the tinfoil around the jar.
6. Make sure the tinfoil is taped.

Enjoy Stars

7. Turn on the smartphone light.
8. Put the smartphone into the jar.
9. Turn off the light in your room.

💬 **Key Expressions**

A : How can I make a star jar?
B : Cut the tinfoil.

Comprehension Check

Read and choose the correct answer.

1. **What is the reading about?**

   a. It's about how to make a star jar.

   b. It's about watching the stars at night.

2. **How can you make stars on the jar?**

   a. I can poke holes in the tinfoil.

   b. I can draw stars on the jar.

3. **To enjoy the stars, you should _____ the light in your room.**

   a. turn on   **b.** turn off

Sentence Focus

Read and choose the correct sentence.

1.
   - [ ] Cut the tinfoil.
   - [ ] Cut the paper clip.

2.
   - [ ] Roll the tinfoil around the jar.
   - [ ] Poke holes in the tinfoil.

3.
   - [ ] Turn on the smartphone light.
   - [ ] Wrap the tinfoil around the jar.

▪ Word Practice ▪

Find, circle, and write the words.

L	K	J	R	Z	W	H	P
D	K	O	J	R	J	O	O
Z	L	M	A	A	D	L	K
L	P	P	L	Z	J	E	E
T	U	R	N	A	D	S	Z
O	F	F	R	O	N	P	Q

jar

⚙ Visualization   Sequence

Use the words in the box to complete the chart. Then, number 1-4 to show the correct order of making the star jar.

Turn on   Poke

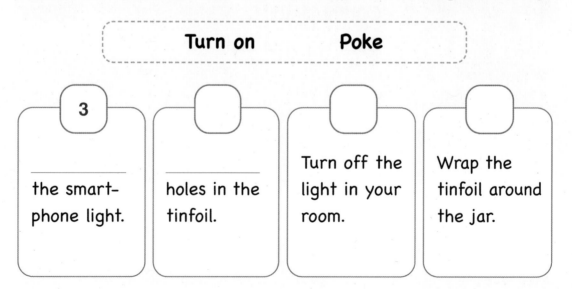

3

_____ the smart-phone light.

_____ holes in the tinfoil.

Turn off the light in your room.

Wrap the tinfoil around the jar.

The Story of Abdul

Talk About It 🎧

1 Do you like chocolate?
2 Do you know how chocolate is made?

▪ Words to Know ▪

Listen and repeat. 🎧

cocoa

farm

harvest

remove

bean

carry

sack

dream

The Story of Abdul 🎧

My name is Abdul.
I am 10 years old.
I work on a cocoa farm.

This is harvest season on the farm.
I wake up early in the morning.
First, I harvest the cocoa pods.
Then, I open the pods and remove the beans.
After that, I carry the bean sack
to the truck.

I work all day long.
It's very hard to work in the heat.

I have a dream.
I want to go to school someday.

Key Expressions

A : What do you do on the
cocoa farm?
B : I harvest the cocoa pods.

▪ Comprehension Check ▪

Read and choose the correct answer.

1. **What is the story about?**

   a. It's about a boy named Abdul.

   b. It's about a cocoa farm.

2. **What does Abdul do on the cocoa farm?**

   a. He harvests the cocoa pods.

   b. He drives the truck.

3. **Abdul _____ of going to school someday.**

   a. works   **b.** dreams

▪ Sentence Focus ▪

Read and choose the correct sentence.

1.
   ☐ I harvest the cocoa pods.
   ☐ I open the cocoa pods.

2.
   ☐ I remove the beans from the pods.
   ☐ I remove the cocoa pods from the sack.

3.
   ☐ I carry the truck.
   ☐ I carry the bean sack.

▪ Word Practice ▪

Find, circle, and write the words.

R	D	M	Y	R	B	T	T
C	E	P	J	L	Z	S	J
J	A	M	M	B	E	A	N
K	J	R	O	V	A	P	X
B	Y	N	R	V	N	E	M
L	J	A	D	Y	E	D	B
G	H	A	R	V	E	S	T

①

②

③

④

_____ _____ _____ _____
remove

💡 Visualization Draw a Conclusion

Use the words in the box to complete the chart.

> farm   school

Abdul is 10 years old.

It's very hard to work on the cocoa _____.

Abdul wants to go to school.

Conclusion

Abdul needs to go to _____ like other children.

86

Working Children

Talk About It 🎧

1 What are the children in the picture doing?
2 Why do you think some children work?

■ Words to Know ■

Listen and repeat. 🎧

children

work

cotton

all day long

sell

sweet

brick

harsh

Working Children 🎧

Many children work.
They work to help their families.
When they work, they don't have time
for other things.

Rosita wants to go to school.
But she has to pick cotton all day long.

Pedro wants to play soccer.
But he has to sell sweets all day long.

Diana wants to learn to read.
But she has to make bricks all day long.

It's too harsh for children to work.
All children need time to enjoy being a child.

Key Expressions

A : What do some children
do to help their families?
B : They pick cotton all day
long.

88

▪ Comprehension Check ▪

Read and choose the correct answer.

1. What is the reading about?

    a. It's about jobs around the world.

    b. It's about children at work.

2. Why do children work?

    a. They work to go to school.

    b. They work to help their families.

3. It's too _____ for children to work all day long.

    a. harsh   **b.** sweet

▪ Sentence Focus ▪

Read and choose the correct sentence.

1.
  ☐ She has to pick cotton all day long.
  ☐ She has to make bricks all day long.

2.
  ☐ He wants to play soccer.
  ☐ He wants to learn to read.

3.
  ☐ They need time to work.
  ☐ They need time to enjoy being a child.

■ Word Practice ■

Find, circle, and write the words.

A	L	S	E	L	L	L	O	W
S	R	H	D	D	Q	D	N	O
D	W	N	A	B	Q	E	B	R
X	N	E	K	R	R	T	P	K
M	Q	P	E	D	S	M	Q	J
T	B	D	L	T	G	H	K	M

harsh

_____   _____   _____   _____

⚙ Visualization   Author's Purpose

Use the words in the box to complete the chart.

work   cotton

Rosita has to pick _____ all day long.	Pedro has to sell sweets all day long.	Diana has to make bricks all day long.

      ↙

Author's Purpose

It's too harsh for children to _____.
All children need time to enjoy being a child.

90

UNIT 01

☐	**twin**	쌍둥이
☐	**same**	같은
☐	**left-handed**	왼손잡이의
☐	**play**	놀다
☐	**ping-pong**	탁구
☐	**tennis**	테니스
☐	**different**	다른
☐	**fingerprint**	지문

UNIT 03

☐	**move**	이사하다
☐	**shell**	소라껍데기
☐	**perfect**	완벽한
☐	**heavy**	무거운
☐	**fancy**	화려한
☐	**plain**	평범한
☐	**find**	찾다
☐	**just right**	딱 알맞은

UNIT 02

☐	**pencil**	연필
☐	**scribble**	휘갈기다
☐	**paper**	종이
☐	**rub**	문지르다
☐	**thumb**	엄지손가락
☐	**tape**	테이프
☐	**put**	붙이다
☐	**press**	누르다

UNIT 04

☐	**home**	집
☐	**houseboat**	선상 집
☐	**family**	가족
☐	**catch**	잡다
☐	**underground house**	지하 집
☐	**cool**	시원한
☐	**heat**	열기
☐	**safe**	안전한

UNIT 05

☐	alone	혼자
☐	busy	바쁜
☐	clean	청소하다
☐	messy	지저분한
☐	pretend	~라고 상상하다
☐	dragon	용
☐	bored	심심해하는
☐	turn	바꾸다

UNIT 06

☐	beat	(게임에서) 이기다
☐	kick	발로 차다
☐	over	끝이 난
☐	miss	빗나가다
☐	upset	마음이 상한
☐	win	이기다
☐	lose	지다
☐	coach	코치

UNIT 07

☐	shiver	떨다
☐	ache	아프다
☐	weak	힘이 없는
☐	put on	(옷을) 입다
☐	sweater	스웨터
☐	muffler	목도리
☐	grandma	할머니
☐	cold	추운

UNIT 08

☐	soup	수프, 국
☐	get over	이겨내다
☐	cold	감기
☐	Asia	아시아
☐	potato	감자
☐	lizard	도마뱀
☐	beef	소고기
☐	feel better	회복하다

UNIT 09

☐	wonder	궁금해하다
☐	lunch	점심식사
☐	river	강
☐	ear	귀
☐	get close	다가가다
☐	bite	깨물다
☐	nose	코
☐	trunk	코끼리의 코

UNIT 10

☐	breathe	숨쉬다
☐	smell	냄새를 맡다
☐	touch	만지다
☐	spray	흩뿌리다
☐	dust	흙
☐	body	몸
☐	pick up	집어들다
☐	protect	보호하다

UNIT 11

☐	**afraid**	두려워하는
☐	**library**	도서관
☐	**gym**	체육관
☐	**tiptoe**	발끝으로 살금살금 걷다
☐	**girl's room**	여자 화장실
☐	**boy's room**	남자 화장실
☐	**locker**	사물함
☐	**shut**	닫다

UNIT 12

☐	**field trip**	현장 학습
☐	**aquarium**	수족관
☐	**kid**	아이
☐	**starfish**	불가사리
☐	**tank**	수조
☐	**shark**	상어
☐	**dangerous**	위험한
☐	**kill**	죽이다, 해치다

UNIT 13

☐	**shoulder**	어깨
☐	**face**	얼굴
☐	**class photo**	학급 사진
☐	**message**	문자 메시지
☐	**hurt**	아프게 하다
☐	**laugh**	웃다
☐	**bully**	(약자를) 괴롭히는 사람
☐	**nice**	좋은

UNIT 14

☐	**etiquette**	예의, 에티켓
☐	**chat**	채팅하다
☐	**comments**	댓글
☐	**social media**	소셜 미디어
☐	**post**	(웹사이트에) 올리다, 게시하다
☐	**true**	사실인
☐	**kind**	친절한
☐	**tag**	태그하다

UNIT 15

☐	**tooth**	이빨, 치아
☐	**flat**	평평한, 고른
☐	**plant**	식물
☐	**sharp**	날카로운
☐	**large**	큰
☐	**front teeth**	앞니
☐	**chew**	씹다
☐	**fight**	싸우다

UNIT 16

☐	**lay an egg**	알을 낳다
☐	**color**	색깔
☐	**young animal**	새끼 동물
☐	**grow**	자라다
☐	**egg tooth**	난치
☐	**break**	깨다
☐	**eggshell**	알 껍데기
☐	**hatch**	부화하다

UNIT 17

☐	**window**	창문
☐	**moon**	달
☐	**miss**	그리워하다
☐	**night**	밤
☐	**street**	거리
☐	**dark**	어두운
☐	**glow**	빛나다
☐	**arrive**	도착하다

UNIT 18

☐	**jar**	단지, 병
☐	**tinfoil**	은박지
☐	**roll**	둥글게 감다
☐	**paper clip**	종이 클립
☐	**poke**	찌르다
☐	**wrap**	싸다
☐	**turn on**	켜다
☐	**turn off**	끄다

UNIT 19

☐	**cocoa**	코코아
☐	**farm**	농장
☐	**harvest**	수확, 수확하다
☐	**remove**	제거하다
☐	**bean**	콩
☐	**carry**	운반하다, 옮기다
☐	**sack**	자루
☐	**dream**	꿈

UNIT 20

☐	**children**	아이들
☐	**work**	일하다
☐	**cotton**	목화
☐	**all day long**	온종일
☐	**sell**	팔다
☐	**sweet**	단 것 (사탕 및 초콜릿류)
☐	**brick**	벽돌
☐	**harsh**	가혹한

리딩 첫걸음부터 완성까지!
초등학생의 영어 성장을 이끄는 4단계 리딩 프로그램

기적의 영어리딩

| 7세~초등 1학년 | 초등 2~3학년 | 초등 4~5학년 | 초등 6학년 이상 |

E2K 지음 │ 30, 50 단계 각 권 13,000원 │ 80, 120 단계 각 권 14,000원

단계	대상	특징	지문당 단어수
기적의 영어리딩 30 (전 3권)	7세~초등 1학년	패턴 문장으로 탄탄한 기초 실력 쌓기	30~40 단어
기적의 영어리딩 50 (전 3권)	초등 2~3학년		50~60 단어
기적의 영어리딩 80 (전 2권)	초등 4~5학년	끊어읽기 연습으로 정확한 독해 완성하기	70~80 단어
기적의 영어리딩 120 (전 2권)	초등 6학년 이상		120~130 단어

교재 특징

1 패턴 문장으로 리딩 첫걸음을 쉽게, 끊어 읽기 연습으로 직독직해 능력 향상!
2 초등 필수 어휘는 물론 리딩 빈출 어휘까지 완벽히 습득
3 워크북과 다양한 부가자료를 활용하여 꼼꼼하고 철저한 복습 가능

길벗스쿨

2.2

미국교과서 리딩

READING

Workbook & Answer Key

R

미국교과서 리딩
READING

LEVEL 2 ②

Workbook

길벗스쿨

We Are Twins

Word Review

A Choose and write.

> same   play   different   fingerprint   ping-pong   left-handed

1.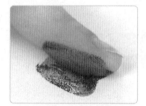

fingerprint

2.

_____

3.

_____

4.

_____

5.

_____

6.

_____

B Read and choose.

1. We are twins.
    b

2. We like to play tennis together.
   [ ]

Sentence Review

A **Read and match.**

1. We like to play

2. We have the same

3. Being a twin is

ⓐ a lot of fun!

ⓑ brown eyes.

ⓒ ping-pong together.

B **Unscramble and write.**

1. | both | We | left-handed. | are |

➜ We are both left-handed.

2. | different | have | We | fingerprints. |

➜

3. | We | have | to play with. | someone | always |

➜

UNIT 02 Fingerprints

Word Review

A Choose and write.

thumb	put	scribble	paper	press	rub

1.

_____

2.

_____

3.

_____

4.

_____

5.

_____

6.

_____

B Read and choose.

1. Take a <u>pencil</u>.

   ☐

2. Now, get some <u>tape</u>.

   ☐

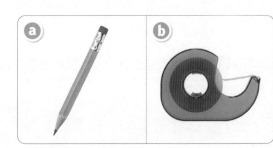

4

Sentence Review

A) Read and match.

1. What do your fingerprints

2. Put a piece of tape

3. Then, rub

a) over your thumb.

b) look like?

c) your thumb.

B) Unscramble and write.

1. these. | Most people's | look like | fingerprints

→

2. put | on a piece of paper. | Then, | the tape

→

3. your thumbprint | does | What | look like?

→

A Perfect Shell

Word Review

A Choose and write.

| fancy | perfect | plain | find | heavy | just right |

1.

_____

2.

_____

3.

_____

4.

_____

5.

_____

6.

_____

B Read and choose.

1. I've found the perfect shell!

☐

2. It's time to move.

☐

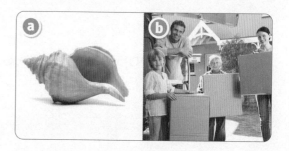

Sentence Review

A Read and match.

1. I've grown too big

2. Is this

3. This shell is

a) the perfect shell?

b) too fancy for me.

c) for my little shell.

B Unscramble and write.

1. | A shell | | just right | | that is | | for me. |

   →

2. | is | | too | | heavy | | for me. | | This shell |

   →

3. | too | | for me. | | is | | This shell | | plain |

   →

Homes Around the World

Word Review

A Choose and write.

| cool | heat | catch | family | safe | houseboat |

1.
_____

2.
_____

3.
_____

4.
_____

5.
_____

6.
_____

B Read and choose.

1. Homes are different around the world.
   ☐

2. He lives in an underground house.
   ☐

8

Sentence Review

A **Read and match.**

1. She lives in

2. It helps his

3. Mongo lives

a) family to live safe.

b) a houseboat.

c) in Mongolia.

B **Unscramble and write.**

1. | lives | She | a yurt. | in |

   →

2. | helps | her family | It | to catch fish | for a living. |

   →

3. | his family | It | to keep cool | helps | from the heat. |

   →

Home Alone

Word Review

A Choose and write.

pretend	bored	busy	clean	turn	messy

1.

_____

2.

_____

3.

_____

4.

_____

5.

_____

6.

_____

B Read and choose.

1. I pretend there's a <u>dragon</u>. ☐

2. I am home alone. ☐

10

Sentence Review

A **Read and match.**

1. All of my friends

2. I'm

3. How can I turn my day

---

a. into a day of fun?

b. are busy.

c. still bored!

B **Unscramble and write.**

1. | clean | my | I | messy | room. |

   →

2. | watch | with | closed. | my eyes | I | TV |

   →

3. | a | day! | What | boring |

   →

Word Review

A **Choose and write.**

| kick | lose | over | miss | beat | coach |

1.
_____

2.
_____

3.
_____

4.
_____

5.
_____

6.
_____

B **Read and choose.**

1. It doesn't matter who <u>wins</u> or <u>loses</u>.
   ☐

2. I was very <u>upset</u>.
   ☐

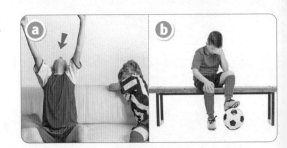

Sentence Review

A **Read and match.**

1. We ran and

2. My shot missed

3. We'll beat

a) the Lion Team today.

b) the net.

c) kicked the ball.

B **Unscramble and write.**

1. almost | The game | was | over.

→

2. kicked | really | I | hard. | the ball

→

3. our | tried | We | best!

→

Achoo!

Word Review

A Choose and write.

| sweater | ache | grandma | cold | weak | put on |

1.

2.

3.

4.

5.

6.

B Read and choose.

1. I put on my muffler.

   ☐

2. I shiver.

   ☐

ⓐ   ⓑ

Sentence Review

A **Read and match.**

1.   My body   **a**   my sweater.

2.   I put on   **b**   aches.

3.   Now, I will not   **c**   be cold anymore.

B **Unscramble and write.**

1. [my] [I] [put on] [hat.]

   →

2. [weak.] [feel] [I] [so]

   →

3. [wrap] [in a blanket.] [I] [myself]

   →

UNIT 08

Soups in Asia

Word Review

A Choose and write.

| lizard | potato | beef | cold | get over | feel better |

1.

_____

2.

_____

3.

_____

4.

_____

5.

_____

6.

_____

B Read and choose.

1. Soups differ around Asia.

   ☐

2. What kind of soup do people in Asia eat?

   ☐

Sentence Review

A **Read and match.**

1. People eat soup

2. People in China eat

3. What do you eat

a. to feel better.

b. to get over a cold?

c. potato soup for a cold.

B **Unscramble and write.**

1. People | eat | in Taiwan | beef noodle soup | for a cold.

→

2. in Hong Kong | lizard soup | People | eat | for a cold.

→

3. eat | to get over | soup | People | a cold.

→

UNIT 09

Why Do Elephants Have Trunks?

A Choose and write.

| lunch | bite | wonder | ear | nose | get close |

1.

_____

2.
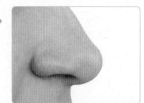
_____

3.

_____

4.

_____

5.

_____

6.

_____

B Read and choose.

1. Elephants have had long trunks.
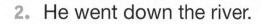
☐

2. He went down the river.
☐

18

Sentence Review

A **Read and match.**

1. What does Mr. Crocodile

2. Little Elephant got close

3. Little Elephant pulled

ⓐ to Mr. Crocodile.

ⓑ eat for lunch?

ⓒ his nose back.

B **Unscramble and write.**

1. | in | tell | I'll | your ear. | you |

→

2. | Little Elephant's nose. | bit | and pulled | Mr. Crocodile |

→

3. | was | from | Little Elephant | Mr. Crocodile. | safe |

→

Elephant Trunk

Word Review

A Choose and write.

| breathe | body | spray | dust | protect | pick up |

1.
_____

2.
_____

3.
_____

4.
_____

5.
_____

6.
_____

B Read and choose.

1. It can use its trunk to <u>touch</u> its baby. ☐

2. They breathe, <u>smell</u>, touch, eat, and drink. ☐

Sentence Review

A **Read and match.**

1. Elephants

2. It can use its trunk

3. They drink

a) to drink water.

b) have long trunks.

c) with their trunks.

B **Unscramble and write.**

1. | Elephants | many things | do | with | their trunks. |

→

2. | itself. | can use | This elephant | to protect | its trunk |

→

3. | This elephant | its trunk | can use | to dig | for water. |

→

We're Not Afraid

Word Review

A Choose and write.

| afraid | locker | tiptoe | library | gym | boy's room |

1.

2.

3.

4.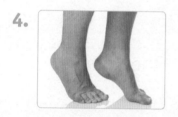

5.

6.

B Read and choose.

1. Back to the girl's room!

2. Shut the door!

22

Sentence Review

A **Read and match.**

1. Is the monster

2. There is a monster

3. We're going on

a inside a locker!

b in the library?

c a monster hunt.

B **Unscramble and write.**

1. [not] [We're] [afraid!]

→

2. [in] [the boy's room?] [it] [Is]

→

3. [not] [We're] [again!] [going on] [a monster hunt]

→

Field Trip

Word Review

A Choose and write.

| kill | shark | tank | aquarium | kid | dangerous |

1.

2.

3.

4.

5.

6.

B Read and choose.

1. We saw starfish in a tank.

2. Today, my class went on a field trip.

a

b

Sentence Review

A **Read and match.**

1. We went to

2. Every kid in the class

3. We had a

ⓐ the aquarium.

ⓑ great day!

ⓒ came on the trip.

B **Unscramble and write.**

1. | saw | box jellyfish. | We |

→

2. | a boy | They | in three minutes! | can kill |

→

3. | I | box jellyfish | very dangerous. | are | learned that |

→

No More Bullies!

Word Review

A Choose and write.

| face | bully | shoulder | hurt | nice | class photo |

1.

_____

2.

_____

3.

_____

4.

_____

5.

_____

6.

_____

B Read and choose.

1. Stevie sent me the same message. ⬜

2. The others laughed at me. ⬜

Sentence Review

A **Read and match.**

1. Nobody

2. Francis pushed me

3. That's not

a. nice!

b. on the shoulder.

c. likes you!

B **Unscramble and write.**

1. | No | | bullies! | | more |

   →

2. | very much. | | hurts | | me | | It |

   →

3. | Jesse | | a big nose | | drew | | in the class photo. | | on my face |

   →

Social Media Etiquette

Word Review

A Choose and write.

| etiquette | comments | chat | tag | true | kind |

1.

_____

2.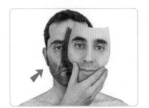

_____

3.

_____

4.

_____

5.

_____

6.

_____

B Read and choose.

1. Think before you post on social media.

   ☐

2. Do you like to chat on social media?

   ☐

Sentence Review

A **Read and match.**

1. Think about if your

   a. hurt your friends.

2. You may

   b. message is true.

3. Think about if it is okay

   c. to tag your friends.

B **Unscramble and write.**

1. | if | Think about | kind. | is | your comment |

   →

2. | to tag | Do | like | you | your friends | on social media? |

   →

3. | dangerous. | Remember that | social media | can be |

   →

Animal Teeth

Word Review

A Choose and write.

tooth	large	plant	sharp	fight	chew

1.

_____

2.

_____

3.

_____

4.

_____

5.

_____

6.

_____

B Read and choose.

1. What large front teeth you have!

2. My flat teeth help me to eat plants.

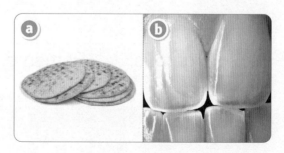

Sentence Review

A **Read and match.**

1. My sharp teeth help

2. I have flat

3. What flat teeth

a. me to eat animals.

b. you have!

c. and sharp teeth.

B **Unscramble and write.**

1. | My | enormous teeth | help | to fight. | me |

→

2. | do | think | I | What | you | eat? |

→

3. | What | have! | teeth | sharp | you |

→

Some Animals Lay Eggs

Word Review

A Choose and write.

| color | grow | eggshell | break | hatch | young animal |

1.

_____

2.

_____

3.

_____

4.

_____

5.

_____

6.

_____

B Read and choose.

1. Some animals lay eggs.

☐

2. Many young animals have an egg tooth.

☐

Sentence Review

A **Read and match.**

1. Young animals grow safely

2. Other animals lay

3. Eggs come in

a) many eggs at once.

b) inside eggs.

c) many different sizes.

B **Unscramble and write.**

1. after | the young animal | The egg tooth | hatches. | falls off

→

2. at a time. | Some animals | just one egg | lay

→

3. come | in many | Eggs | colors. | different

→

Night Walk

Word Review

A Choose and write.

| miss | street | window | glow | arrive | night |

1.

2.

3.

4.

5.

6.

B Read and choose.

1. I see the <u>moon</u>.

2. It is <u>dark</u> outside.

 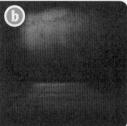

Sentence Review

A) Read and match.

1. I look out

2. Dad and I walk out

3. Stars shine even

a) in the night.

b) brighter today!

c) the window.

B) Unscramble and write.

1. | go | Can | and see | I | her | now? |

   →

2. | Grandma | of the street. | on the other side | lives |

   →

3. | walk | glowing | and see | We | in the dark. | something |

   →

Star Jar

Word Review

A Choose and write.

jar	poke	roll	wrap	paper clip	turn on

1.
_____

2.
_____

3.
_____

4.
_____

5.
_____

6.
_____

B Read and choose.

1. Turn off the light in your room.
   ☐

2. Cut the tinfoil.
   ☐

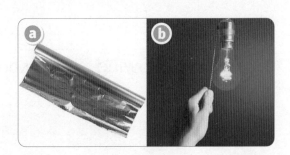

Sentence Review

A **Read and match.**

1. Poke as many holes

2. Let's make a

3. Make sure

a   as you want.

b   the tinfoil is taped.

c   star jar.

B **Unscramble and write.**

1. | the smartphone | | Turn on | | light. |

   →

2. | the tinfoil | | the jar. | | around | | Wrap |

   →

3. | a jar | | Take | | and roll | | around | | it. | | tinfoil |

   →

The Story of Abdul

Word Review

A Choose and write.

| farm | cocoa | carry | sack | bean | remove |

1. _____

2. _____

3. _____

4. _____

5. _____

6. _____

B Read and choose.

1. This is <u>harvest</u> season on the farm.

2. I have a <u>dream</u>.

Sentence Review

A **Read and match.**

1. I wake up early   a   a cocoa farm.

2. I work on   b   in the morning.

3. It's very hard to   c   work in the heat.

B **Unscramble and write.**

1. | all day long. | | work | | I |

   →

2. | the bean sack | | to the truck. | | I | | carry |

   →

3. | want | | to school | | I | | someday. | | to go |

   →

Working Children

Word Review

A Choose and write.

| sell | work | cotton | sweet | brick | harsh |

1.
_ _ _ _ _ _ _ _

2.
_ _ _ _ _ _ _ _

3.
_ _ _ _ _ _ _ _

4.
_ _ _ _ _ _ _ _

5.
_ _ _ _ _ _ _ _

6.
_ _ _ _ _ _ _ _

B Read and choose.

1. Many children work.

2. She has to pick cotton all day long.

Sentence Review

A **Read and match.**

1. He has to sell

2. It's too harsh

3. Diana wants

a. for children to work.

b. to learn to read.

c. sweets all day long.

B **Unscramble and write.**

1. | to play | wants | soccer. | Pedro |

→

2. | make | all day long. | She | bricks | has to |

→

3. | work | They | to help | their families. |

→

Unit 01. We Are Twins

Word Review Ⓑ **1.** ⓑ **2.** ⓐ

Sentence Review

Ⓐ **1.** ⓒ **2.** ⓑ **3.** ⓐ

Ⓑ **1.** We are both left-handed.
2. We have different fingerprints.
3. We always have someone to play with.

Unit 02. Fingerprints

Word Review Ⓑ **1.** ⓐ **2.** ⓑ

Sentence Review

Ⓐ **1.** ⓑ **2.** ⓐ **3.** ⓒ

Ⓑ **1.** Most people's fingerprints look like these.
2. Then, put the tape on a piece of paper.
3. What does your thumbprint look like?

Unit 03. A Perfect Shell

Word Review Ⓑ **1.** ⓐ **2.** ⓑ

Sentence Review

Ⓐ **1.** ⓒ **2.** ⓐ **3.** ⓑ

Ⓑ **1.** A shell that is just right for me.
2. This shell is too heavy for me.
3. This shell is too plain for me.

Unit 04. Homes Around the World

Word Review Ⓑ **1.** ⓑ **2.** ⓐ

Sentence Review

Ⓐ **1.** ⓑ **2.** ⓐ **3.** ⓒ

Ⓑ **1.** She lives in a yurt.
2. It helps her family to catch fish for a living.
3. It helps his family to keep cool from the heat.

Unit 05. Home Alone

Word Review Ⓑ **1.** ⓑ **2.** ⓐ

Sentence Review

Ⓐ **1.** ⓑ **2.** ⓒ **3.** ⓐ

Ⓑ **1.** I clean my messy room.
2. I watch TV with my eyes closed.
3. What a boring day!

Unit 06. Big Game

Word Review Ⓑ **1.** ⓐ **2.** ⓑ

Sentence Review

Ⓐ **1.** ⓒ **2.** ⓑ **3.** ⓐ

Ⓑ **1.** The game was almost over.
2. I kicked the ball really hard.
3. We tried our best!

Unit 07. Achoo!

Word Review Ⓑ **1.** ⓑ **2.** ⓐ

Sentence Review

Ⓐ **1.** ⓑ **2.** ⓐ **3.** ⓒ

Ⓑ **1.** I put on my hat.
2. I feel so weak.
3. I wrap myself in a blanket.

Unit 08. Soups in Asia

Word Review Ⓑ **1.** ⓐ **2.** ⓑ

Sentence Review

Ⓐ **1.** ⓐ **2.** ⓒ **3.** ⓑ

Ⓑ **1.** People in Taiwan eat beef noodle soup for a cold.
  2. People in Hong Kong eat lizard soup for a cold.
  3. People eat soup to get over a cold.

Unit 09. Why Do Elephants Have Trunks?

Word Review Ⓑ **1.** ⓐ **2.** ⓑ

Sentence Review

Ⓐ **1.** ⓑ **2.** ⓐ **3.** ⓒ

Ⓑ **1.** I'll tell you in your ear.
  2. Mr. Crocodile bit and pulled Little Elephant's nose.
  3. Little Elephant was safe from Mr. Crocodile.

Unit 10. Elephant Trunk

Word Review Ⓑ **1.** ⓑ **2.** ⓐ

Sentence Review

Ⓐ **1.** ⓑ **2.** ⓐ **3.** ⓒ

Ⓑ **1.** Elephants do many things with their trunks.
  2. This elephant can use its trunk to protect itself.
  3. This elephant can use its trunk to dig for water.

Unit 11. We're Not Afraid

Word Review Ⓑ **1.** ⓐ **2.** ⓑ

Sentence Review

Ⓐ **1.** ⓑ **2.** ⓐ **3.** ⓒ

Ⓑ **1.** We're not afraid!
  2. Is it in the boy's room?
  3. We're not going on a monster hunt again!

Unit 12. Field Trip

Word Review Ⓑ **1.** ⓐ **2.** ⓑ

Sentence Review

Ⓐ **1.** ⓐ **2.** ⓒ **3.** ⓑ

Ⓑ **1.** We saw box jellyfish.
  2. They can kill a boy in three minutes!
  3. I learned that box jellyfish are very dangerous.

Unit 13. No More Bullies!

Word Review Ⓑ **1.** ⓑ **2.** ⓐ

Sentence Review

Ⓐ **1.** ⓒ **2.** ⓑ **3.** ⓐ

Ⓑ **1.** No more bullies!
  2. It hurts me very much.
  3. Jesse drew a big nose on my face in the class photo.

Unit 14. Social Media Etiquette

Word Review Ⓑ **1.** ⓐ **2.** ⓑ

Sentence Review

Ⓐ **1.** ⓑ **2.** ⓐ **3.** ⓒ

Ⓑ **1.** Think about if your comment is kind.
  2. Do you like to tag your friends on social media?
  3. Remember that social media can be dangerous.

Unit 15. Animal Teeth

Word Review Ⓑ **1.** ⓑ **2.** ⓐ

Sentence Review

Ⓐ **1.** ⓐ **2.** ⓒ **3.** ⓑ

Ⓑ **1.** My enormous teeth help me to fight.
2. What do you think I eat?
3. What sharp teeth you have!

Unit 16. Some Animals Lay Eggs

Word Review Ⓑ **1.** ⓐ **2.** ⓑ

Sentence Review

Ⓐ **1.** ⓑ **2.** ⓐ **3.** ⓒ

Ⓑ **1.** The egg tooth falls off after the young animal hatches.
2. Some animals lay just one egg at a time.
3. Eggs come in many different colors.

Unit 17. Night Walk

Word Review Ⓑ **1.** ⓐ **2.** ⓑ
Sentence Review

Ⓐ **1.** ⓒ **2.** ⓐ **3.** ⓑ

Ⓑ **1.** Can I go and see her now?
2. Grandma lives on the other side of the street.
3. We walk and see something glowing in the dark.

Unit 18. Star Jar

Word Review Ⓑ **1.** ⓑ **2.** ⓐ
Sentence Review

Ⓐ **1.** ⓐ **2.** ⓒ **3.** ⓑ

Ⓑ **1.** Turn on the smartphone light.
2. Wrap the tinfoil around the jar.
3. Take a jar and roll tinfoil around it.

Unit 19. The Story of Abdul

Word Review Ⓑ **1.** ⓐ **2.** ⓑ
Sentence Review

Ⓐ **1.** ⓑ **2.** ⓐ **3.** ⓒ

Ⓑ **1.** I work all day long.
2. I carry the bean sack to the truck.
3. I want to go to school someday.

Unit 20. Working Children

Word Review Ⓑ **1.** ⓑ **2.** ⓐ
Sentence Review

Ⓐ **1.** ⓒ **2.** ⓐ **3.** ⓑ

Ⓑ **1.** Pedro wants to play soccer.
2. She has to make bricks all day long.
3. They work to help their families.

미국교과서 리딩 READING

LEVEL 2 ②

Answer Key

Talk About It

- 사진 속의 쌍둥이를 잘 살펴보세요. 그들은 어떻게 닮았나요?
- 그들은 어떻게 다른가요?

Words to Know

듣고 따라 말해 보세요.

- twin 쌍둥이
- left-handed 왼손잡이의
- ping-pong 탁구
- different 다른
- same 같은
- play 놀다
- tennis 테니스
- fingerprint 지문

Main Reading

우리는 쌍둥이예요.
우리는 같은 갈색 눈을 가지고 있어요.
우리 둘 다 왼손잡이예요.
때로는 우리 엄마도 우리를 구분하지 못해요!
쌍둥이인 것은 정말 재미있어요!
우리는 항상 같이 놀 친구가 있는 셈이지요.
우리는 같이 탁구 치는 것을 좋아해요.
우리는 함께 테니스 치는 것을 좋아해요.
우리를 다르게 만들어주는 것이 딱 하나 있죠.
우리는 지문이 달라요.
차이점을 구별할 수 있나요?

Key Expressions

A: 너희들은 어떻게 닮았니?
B: 우리는 같은 파란 눈을 가졌어.

| 문제 정답 및 해설 |

Comprehension Check

읽고 알맞은 답을 고르세요.

1. 무엇에 관한 글인가요? [정답 : b]
  a. 운동 경기에 관한 글이에요.
  b. 쌍둥이에 관한 글이에요.

2. 왜 가끔씩 엄마는 우리가 누구인지 구분하지 못할까요? [정답 : a]
  a. 우리가 같은 갈색 눈동자를 가졌기 때문이에요.
  b. 우리가 다른 지문을 가졌기 때문이에요.

3. 우리의 지문은 우리를 달라보이게 만듭니다. [정답 : b]
  a. 눈의 색깔
  b. 지문

Sentence Focus

읽고 알맞은 문장을 고르세요.

1. ■ 우리는 다른 지문을 가졌어요.
  □ 우리는 다른 눈동자 색을 가졌어요.

2. □ 우리는 함께 축구 하는 것을 좋아해요.
  ■ 우리는 함께 탁구 치는 것을 좋아해요.

3. ■ 쌍둥이인 것은 정말 재미있어요!
  □ 서로 다른 것은 정말 재미있어요!

Word Practice

그림에 알맞은 단어를 찾아 동그라미 하고 써 보세요.

1. same **2.** different **3.** twin **4.** fingerprint

F	I	N	G	E	R	P	R	I	N	T
D	I	F	F	E	R	E	N	T	W	B
E	M	B	S	A	M	E	M	I	R	L
X	Y	W	D	Y	D	M	N	Q	Q	N

Visualization : 비교와 대조

주어진 단어를 이용해서 표를 완성하세요.

- (순서대로) tennis / brown
- 다른 점 – 지문
- 같은 점 – 갈색 눈, 왼손잡이, 탁구 치는 것을 좋아해요, 테니스 치는 것을 좋아해요.

Talk About It

- 사진 속의 사람은 무엇을 하고 있나요?
- 지문은 왜 중요할까요?

Words to Know

듣고 따라 말해 보세요.

- pencil 연필
- paper 종이
- thumb 엄지손가락
- put 붙이다
- scribble 휘갈기다
- rub 문지르다
- tape 테이프
- press 누르다

Main Reading

당신의 지문은 어떻게 생겼나요?
그 어떤 두 개의 지문도 완전히 똑같지는 않아요.
하지만 대부분 사람들의 지문은 이렇게 생겼어요.

- 소용돌이형 지문   · 고리형 지문   · 아치형 지문

연필을 하나 꺼내서 종이 한 장 위에 휘갈겨 써 보세요.
그런 다음, 엄지손가락을 문지르세요.
이제 테이프를 좀 가져오세요.
테이프 한 조각을 엄지손가락 위에 붙이고,
꾹 누른 다음 떼어내세요.
그런 다음, 그 테이프를 종이 한 장 위에 붙이세요.
당신의 엄지손가락 지문은 어떻게 생겼나요?

Key Expressions

A: 네 엄지손가락 지문은 어떻게 생겼니?
B: 소용돌이 모양 같아 보여.

| 문제 정답 및 해설 |

Comprehension Check

읽고 알맞은 답을 고르세요.

1. 무엇에 관한 글인가요?   [정답 : a]
   a. 지문에 관한 글이에요.
   b. 엄지손가락에 관한 글이에요.

2. 테이프를 가져오기 전에 무엇을 해야 하나요?   [정답 : a]
   a. 종이 위에 엄지손가락을 문질러야 해요.
   b. 엄지손가락 위에 테이프를 붙여야 해요.

3. 그 어떤 두 개의 지문도 완전히 똑같지 않아요.   [정답 : b]
   a. 테이프   b. 지문

Sentence Focus

읽고 알맞은 문장을 고르세요.

1. ■ 어떤 사람들의 지문은 소용돌이 모양이에요.
   □ 어떤 사람들의 지문은 고리 모양이에요.

2. □ 종이 한 장을 가져오세요.
   ■ 종이 한 장 위에 휘갈겨 쓰세요.

3. □ 그 테이프를 엄지손가락 위에 붙이세요.
   ■ 그 테이프를 종이 한 장 위에 붙이세요.

Word Practice

그림에 알맞은 단어를 찾아 동그라미 하고 써 보세요.

1. rub   **2.** pencil   **3.** put   **4.** thumb

P	M	J	T	B	J	T
E	J	N	R	P	H	R
N	Z	N	Y	U	U	P
C	Z	L	M	B	Y	T
I	X	B	D	J	Z	R
L	T	W	N	B	N	Z

Visualization : 주제와 세부사항

주어진 단어를 이용해서 표를 완성하세요.

- (순서대로) Fingerprints / tape
- 주제 – 지문
- 세부사항 – 그 어떤 두 개의 지문도 완전히 똑같지는 않아요.
  – 대부분 사람들의 지문은 소용돌이, 고리, 아치 모양이에요.
  – 지문을 찍기 위해서 연필 한 자루, 테이프, 종이가 필요해요.

Talk About It

• 당신은 소라게에 대해 무엇을 알고 있나요?

• 소라게는 등 위에 무엇을 가지고 다니나요?

Words to Know

듣고 따라 말해 보세요.

• move 이사하다

• perfect 완벽한

• fancy 화려한

• find 찾다

• shell 소라껍데기

• heavy 무거운

• plain 평범한

• just right 딱 알맞은

Main Reading

이사할 시간이에요.

나는 내 작은 소라껍데기에 비해 너무 크게 자랐어요.

이것이 완벽한 소라껍데기일까요?

아뇨, 이 소라껍데기는 나에게 너무 커요.

이것이 완벽한 소라껍데기일까요?

아뇨, 이 소라껍데기는 나에게 너무 무거워요.

이것이 완벽한 소라껍데기일까요?

아뇨, 이 소라껍데기는 나에게 너무 화려해요.

이것이 완벽한 소라껍데기일까요?

아뇨, 이 소라껍데기는 나에게 너무 평범해요.

완벽한 소라껍데기를 찾았어요!

나에게 딱 맞는 소라껍데기예요.

• 소라게

Key Expressions

A: 이것이 완벽한 소라껍데기니?

B: 아니, 이 소라껍데기는 나에게 너무 커.

| 문제 정답 및 해설 |

Comprehension Check

읽고 알맞은 답을 고르세요.

1. 나는 누구인가요? [정답 : b]

   a. 나는 소라껍데기입니다.   **b.** 나는 소라게입니다.

2. 나는 왜 이사를 해야 하나요? [정답 : a]

   a. 내가 너무 크게 자랐기 때문이에요.

   b. 내 소라껍데기가 너무 무겁기 때문이에요.

3. 나는 <u>완벽한</u> 소라껍데기를 찾고 있어요. [정답 : b]

   a. 큰   **b.** 완벽한

Sentence Focus

읽고 알맞은 문장을 고르세요.

1. ■ 이 소라껍데기는 나에게 너무 무거워요.

   □ 이 소라껍데기는 나에게 너무 작아요.

2. □ 이 소라껍데기는 나에게 너무 화려해요.

   ■ 이 소라껍데기는 나에게 너무 평범해요.

3. □ 나는 무거운 소라껍데기를 찾았어요!

   ■ 나는 완벽한 소라껍데기를 찾았어요!

Word Practice

그림에 알맞은 단어를 찾아 동그라미 하고 써 보세요.

1. shell   **2.** heavy   **3.** find   **4.** just right

J	U	S	T	R	I	G	H	T
F	X	H	R	S	T	J	T	D
I	L	P	E	M	H	Q	R	P
N	J	J	M	A	D	E	B	L
D	W	Z	N	L	V	X	L	K
X	X	Y	M	V	R	Y	M	L

Visualization : 원인과 결과

주어진 단어를 이용해서 표를 완성하세요.

• (순서대로) <u>move</u> / <u>perfect</u>

왜인가요?	무슨 일이 일어났나요?
– 나는 내 작은 소라껍데기에 비해 너무 크게 자랐어요.	⇨ <u>이사할</u> 시간이에요.
– 이 소라껍데기는 나에게 딱 맞아요.	⇨ 이것이 <u>완벽한</u> 소라껍데기예요.

Talk About It

• 당신은 어디에 살고 있나요?
• 당신의 집은 당신이 생활하는 데 어떤 도움을 주나요?

Words to Know

듣고 따라 말해 보세요.

• home 집
• family 가족
• underground house 지하 집
• heat 열기

• houseboat 선상 집
• catch 잡다
• cool 시원한
• safe 안전한

Main Reading

세계 각지의 집들은 모두 달라요.
루디는 태국에 살아요.
그녀는 선상 집에 살고 있지요.
그 집은 그녀의 가족이 생계를 위해 물고기를 잡을 수 있도록 도와줘요.
아지즈는 튀니지에 살아요.
그는 지하 집에 살고 있어요.
그 집은 그의 가족이 열기로부터 시원하게 지낼 수 있게 도와주죠.
몽고는 몽골에 살아요.
그녀는 유르트에서 살고 있지요.
그 집은 그녀의 가족이 어디든 가고 싶은 곳으로 갈 수 있게 도와줘요.
알라는 난민 캠프에 살아요.
그는 텐트에서 살고 있지요.
그 집은 그의 가족이 안전하게 지낼 수 있게 도와줘요.
(위부터) • 선상 집 • 지하 집   • 유르트

Key Expressions

A: 너는 어디에 사니?
B: 나는 선상 집에서 살아.

문제 정답 및 해설 |

Comprehension Check

읽고 알맞은 답을 고르세요.

• 무엇에 관한 글인가요?   [정답 : a]
    a. 집들에 관한 글이에요.

b. 세계에 관한 글이에요.

2. 유르트는 몽고의 가족을 어떻게 도와주나요?   [정답 : b]
    a. 그들이 안전하게 지내도록 도와줘요.
    b. 그들이 원하는 어디든 갈 수 있게 해줘요.

3. 사람들은 다른 종류의 집에서 살아요.   [정답 : a]
    a. 집   b. 텐트

Sentence Focus

읽고 알맞은 문장을 고르세요.

1. ■ 그녀는 지하 집에 살아요.
   □ 그녀는 유르트에서 살아요.

2. ■ 그것은 그녀의 가족이 생계를 위해 물고기를 잡도록 도와줘요.
   □ 그것은 그녀의 가족이 열기로부터 시원하게 지내도록 도와줘요.

3. □ 알라는 선상 집에 살아요.
   ■ 알라는 난민 캠프에 살아요.

Word Practice

그림에 알맞은 단어를 찾아 동그라미 하고 써 보세요.

1. family   **2.** home   **3.** catch   **4.** safe

```
F C A T C H B
Q A Q S E W T
H M M M A L T
O Y O I Y F V
M L W W L D E
E B Z T Y Y J
```

Visualization : 주제와 세부사항

주어진 단어를 이용해서 표를 완성하세요.

· (순서대로) houseboat / tent
· 세계 각지의 집들은 달라요.
· 태국 – 선상 집   · 튀니지 – 지하 집
· 몽골 – 유르트   · 난민 캠프 – 텐트

Talk About It

- 당신은 집에 혼자 있어본 적이 있나요?
- 당신은 집에 혼자 있는 것을 좋아하나요?

Words to Know

듣고 따라 말해 보세요.

- alone 혼자
- busy 바쁜
- clean 청소하다
- messy 지저분한
- pretend ~라고 상상하다
- dragon 용
- bored 심심해하는
- turn 바꾸다

Main Reading

나는 집에 혼자 있어요.
내 친구들은 모두 바빠요.
나는 지저분한 내 방을 청소해요.
나는 샴푸로 비눗방울을 만들어요.
내가 가장 좋아하는 책도 읽죠.
나는 용이 있는 것처럼 상상해요.
나는 눈을 감고 TV를 봐요.
여전히 심심하네요!
어떻게 하면 나의 하루를 재미있는 날로 바꿀 수 있을까요?
재미있게 할 일이 하나도 생각이 안 나요.
정말 지루한 날이에요!

Key Expressions

A: 너는 무엇을 하고 있니?
B: 나는 지저분한 내 방을 청소하는 중이야.

| 문제 정답 및 해설 |

Comprehension Check

읽고 알맞은 답을 고르세요.

1. 나는 왜 집에 혼자 있나요?   [정답 : b]
   a. 해야할 일이 많기 때문이에요.
   b. 친구들이 모두 바쁘기 때문이에요.

2. 나의 문제는 무엇인가요?   [정답 : a]
   a. 나는 심심해요.
   b. 나는 아파요.

3. 나는 나의 하루를 재미있는 날로 <u>바꾸고</u> 싶어요.   [정답 : b]
   a. 생각하다   **b.** 바꾸다

Sentence Focus

읽고 알맞은 문장을 고르세요.

1. ■ 나는 집에 혼자 있어요.
   □ 나는 친구들과 함께 집에 있어요.

2. □ 나는 지저분한 내 방을 청소해요.
   ■ 나는 내가 가장 좋아하는 책을 읽어요.

3. □ 정말 바쁜 날이에요!
   ■ 정말 지루한 날이에요!

Word Practice

그림에 알맞은 단어를 찾아 동그라미 하고 써 보세요.

1. alone   **2.** busy   **3.** clean   **4.** messy

Visualization : 문제점과 해결책

주어진 단어를 이용해서 표를 완성하세요.

- (왼쪽부터) <u>bored</u> / <u>pretend</u>
- 문제점 – 나는 <u>심심해요</u>.
- 해결책 – 나는 용이 <u>있다고</u> <u>상상해요</u>.
    – 나는 샴푸로 비눗방울을 만들어요.

Talk About It

- 당신이 가장 좋아하는 스포츠는 무엇인가요?
- 당신은 왜 그 스포츠를 좋아하나요?

Words to Know

듣고 따라 말해 보세요.

- beat (게임에서) 이기다
- over 끝이 난
- upset 마음이 상한
- lose 지다
- kick 발로 차다
- miss 빗나가다
- win 이기다
- coach 코치

Main Reading

오늘은 중요한 경기가 있어요.
우리는 오늘 라이언 팀을 이길 거예요.
우리는 달리고 공을 찼어요.
경기가 거의 끝났어요.
나는 공을 아주 세게 찼어요.
하지만 내 슛이 골대를 빗나가고 말았지요.
내가 너무 높이 찼던 거예요.
라이언 팀이 경기를 이겼어요.
난 몹시 마음이 상했죠.
"누가 이기고 지는지는 중요하지 않단다."라고 감독님이 말씀하셨어요.
"맞아, 잭! 우리는 최선을 다했잖아!" 타이거 팀은 행복하게 외쳤답니다.

Key Expressions

A: 너는 오늘 무엇을 했니?
B: 나는 달리고 공을 찼어.

| 문제 정답 및 해설 |

Comprehension Check

읽고 알맞은 답을 고르세요.

1. 무엇에 관한 글인가요?   [정답 : a]
   a. 중요한 경기에 관한 글이에요.
   b. 라이언 팀에 관한 글이에요.

2. 나는 왜 마음이 몹시 상했나요?   [정답 : a]

    a. 라이언 팀이 경기에서 이겼기 때문이에요.
    b. 우리가 라이언 팀을 이겼기 때문이에요.

3. 사진 속에서, 아이들은 축구를 하고 있어요.   [정답 : b]
    a. 농구   b. 축구

Sentence Focus

읽고 알맞은 문장을 고르세요.

1. □ 우리는 오늘 경기에서 질 거예요.
   ■ 우리는 오늘 경기에서 이길 거예요.

2. ■ 나는 공을 아주 세게 찼어요.
   □ 내 슛이 골대를 빗나갔어요.

3. ■ 나는 몹시 마음이 상했어요.
   □ 우리는 최선을 다했어요.

Word Practice

그림에 알맞은 단어를 찾아 동그라미 하고 써 보세요.

1. kick   2. win   3. coach   4. lose

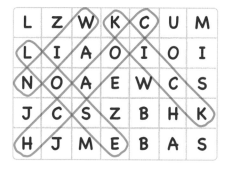

Visualization : 이야기의 구성 요소

주어진 단어를 이용해서 표를 완성하세요.

· (왼쪽부터) upset / missed

누가?	어떻게 느꼈나요?	왜인가요?
– 나	– 매우 속상한	– 내 슛이 골대를 벗어났어요. 라이언 팀이 이겼어요.
– 타이거 팀과 나	– 행복한	– 우리는 최선을 다했어요.

Talk About It

- 당신은 감기에 걸리면 어떤 느낌인가요?
- 당신은 감기에 걸렸을 때 무엇을 하나요?

Words to Know

듣고 따라 말해 보세요.

- shiver 떨다
- weak 힘이 없는
- sweater 스웨터
- grandma 할머니
- ache 아프다
- put on 입다
- muffler 목도리
- cold 추운

Main Reading

몸이 떨려요.
몸이 아파요.
나는 몹시 기운이 없어요. 에취!
나는 모자를 써요.
스웨터를 입어요.
목도리를 둘러요.
그리고 담요로 내 몸을 감싸요.
할머니가 오셔서 말씀하셔요.
"이것이 도움이 될 거란다, 아가야."
난 외쳐요. "우와, 닭고기 수프네요!"
만세!
이제 난 더이상 춥지 않을 거예요.
할머니의 닭고기 수프는 언제나 맛있어요.

Key Expressions

A: 너는 감기에 걸리면 어떤 느낌이니?
B: 나는 춥다고 느껴.

| 문제 정답 및 해설 |

Comprehension Check

읽고 알맞은 답을 고르세요.

1. 나에게 어떤 문제가 있나요? [정답 : a]
   a. 몸이 떨리고 아파요.
   b. 나는 담요로 몸을 감싸요.

2. 할머니는 나를 위해 무엇을 해주시나요? [정답 : b]
   a. 내가 스웨터 입는 것을 도와주세요.
   b. 나를 위해 닭고기 수프를 만들어 주세요.

3. 나는 할머니의 닭고기 수프를 좋아해요. [정답 : b]
   a. 나의 담요   b. 할머니의 닭고기 수프

Sentence Focus

읽고 알맞은 문장을 고르세요.

1. ☐ 나는 기분이 정말 좋아요.
   ■ 나는 몹시 기운이 없어요.

2. ■ 나는 모자를 써요.
   ☐ 나는 목도리를 둘러요.

3. ☐ 할머니의 스웨터는 멋져요.
   ■ 할머니의 닭고기 수프는 정말 맛있어요.

Word Practice

그림에 알맞은 단어를 찾아 동그라미 하고 써 보세요.

1. weak   2. sweater   3. put on   4. ache

S	W	E	A	T	E	R
A	W	P	U	T	O	N
C	E	E	Z	D	W	B
H	N	A	A	K	V	L
E	X	N	K	K	J	M

Visualization : 원인과 결과

주어진 단어를 이용해서 표를 완성하세요.

- (순서대로) shiver / Grandma

왜인가요?	무슨 일이 일어났나요?
– 나는 몸이 떨려요.	⇨ 나는 담요로 내 몸을 감싸요.
– 나는 할머니의 닭고기 수프를 먹어요.	⇨ 나는 더이상 춥지 않을 거예요.

Talk About It

- 당신은 감기를 어떻게 이겨내나요?
- 당신은 감기 때문에 특별한 것을 먹나요?

Words to Know

듣고 따라 말해 보세요.

- soup 수프
- cold 감기
- potato 감자
- beef 소고기
- get over 이겨내다
- Asia 아시아
- lizard 도마뱀
- feel better 회복하다

Main Reading

사람들은 감기를 이겨내기 위해서 수프를 먹어요.
아시아의 사람들은 어떤 종류의 수프를 먹을까요?
중국 사람들은 감기에 감자 수프를 먹어요.
홍콩 사람들은 감기에 도마뱀 수프를 먹죠.
일본 사람들은 감기에 된장국을 먹어요.
한국 사람들은 감기에 콩나물국을 먹죠.
대만 사람들은 감기에 소고기 국수를 먹어요.
태국 사람들은 감기에 닭고기 쌀죽을 먹죠.
아시아 곳곳의 수프는 달라요.
하지만 사람들은 빨리 낫기 위해 수프를 먹어요.
(왼쪽 사진부터) • 소고기 국수 • 감자 수프 • 된장국

Key Expressions

A: 너는 감기를 이겨내기 위해 무엇을 먹니?
B: 나는 닭고기 수프를 먹어.

| 문제 정답 및 해설 |

Comprehension Check

읽고 알맞은 답을 고르세요.

1. 무엇에 관한 글인가요?　　　　　　　　　[정답 : a]
　a. 감기를 위한 아시아의 수프에 관한 글이에요.
　b. 아시아 사람들이 가장 좋아하는 수프에 관한 글이에요.

2. 홍콩 사람들은 감기에 무엇을 먹나요?　　　[정답 : b]
　a. 감자 수프를 먹어요.
　b. 도마뱀 수프를 먹어요.

3. 사람들은 <u>감기</u>를 이겨내기 위해 다른 수프를 먹어요.　[정답 : a]
　a. 감기　　　**b.** 통증

Sentence Focus

읽고 알맞은 문장을 고르세요.

1. ■ 아시아 곳곳의 수프는 달라요.
　　□ 아시아 곳곳의 국수는 달라요.

2. ■ 대만 사람들은 소고기 국수를 먹어요.
　　□ 중국 사람들은 감자 수프를 먹어요.

3. ■ 사람들은 감기를 이겨내기 위해 수프를 먹어요.
　　□ 사람들은 감기를 이겨내기 위해 빵을 먹어요.

Word Practice

그림에 알맞은 단어를 찾아 동그라미 하고 써 보세요.

1. soup　**2.** beef　**3.** potato　**4.** feel better

F	E	E	L	B	E	T	T	E	R
P	O	T	A	T	O	J	T	S	J
Q	K	L	B	X	B	V	O	Z	W
Z	G	E	M	M	Y	U	M	P	D
D	E	Y	T	D	P	D	X	Q	B
F	B	M	J	L	N	Y	W	Y	W

Visualization : 주제와 세부사항

주어진 단어를 이용해서 표를 완성하세요.

- (순서대로) <u>get over</u> / <u>Asia</u>
- 주제 – 감기에 먹는 아시아의 수프
- 세부사항 – 사람들은 감기를 <u>이겨내기</u> 위해 수프를 먹어요.
　　　　　 – <u>아시아</u> 곳곳의 수프는 달라요.

Talk About It

- 사진을 보세요. 그들은 어떻게 닮았나요?
- 그들은 어떻게 다른가요?

Words to Know

듣고 따라 말해 보세요.

- wonder 궁금해하다
- river 강
- get close 다가가다
- nose 코
- lunch 점심식사
- ear 귀
- bite 깨물다
- trunk 코끼리의 코

Main Reading

옛날에, 꼬마 코끼리가 살았어요.
어느날 아침, 꼬마 코끼리는 궁금했어요.
"악어 아저씨는 점심식사로 무엇을 드실까?"
그는 답을 찾기 위해 강을 따라 내려갔죠.
"악어 아저씨, 아저씨는 점심식사로 무엇을 드세요?"
"이리 오렴, 아가야. 네 귀에 대고 얘기해줄게."
꼬마 코끼리는 악어 아저씨에게 가까이 다가갔어요.
악어 아저씨는 꼬마 코끼리의 코를 물고는 잡아당겼어요.
꼬마 코끼리는 자신의 코를 뒤로 당겼죠.
꼬마 코끼리는 악어 아저씨로부터 안전하게 벗어났어요.
그때부터, 코끼리들은 긴 코를 갖게 되었답니다.

Key Expressions

A: 꼬마 코끼리는 무엇을 했어?
B: 그는 강을 따라 내려갔어.

| 문제 정답 및 해설 |

Comprehension Check

읽고 알맞은 답을 고르세요.

1. 누구에 관한 이야기인가요? [정답 : b]
   a. 악어 아저씨에 관한 이야기예요.
   b. 꼬마 코끼리에 관한 이야기예요.

2. 꼬마 코끼리는 왜 강을 따라 내려갔나요? [정답 : a]
   a. 악어 아저씨가 점심식사로 무엇을 먹는지 알아내기 위해서
   b. 악어 아저씨가 점심에 무엇을 하는지 알아내기 위해서

3. 악어 아저씨는 꼬마 코끼리의 코를 물었어요. [정답 : b]
   a. 귀   **b.** 코

Sentence Focus

읽고 알맞은 문장을 고르세요.

1. ☐ 그는 점심을 먹기 위해 강을 내려갔어요.
   ■ 그는 악어 아저씨를 만나기 위해 강을 내려갔어요.

2. ■ 내가 너의 귀에 대고 얘기해줄게.
   ☐ 내가 너의 코에 대고 얘기해줄게.

3. ☐ 코끼리는 짧은 코를 가지고 있어요.
   ■ 코끼리는 긴 코를 가지고 있어요.

Word Practice

그림에 알맞은 단어를 찾아 동그라미 하고 써 보세요.

1. nose **2.** get close **3.** river **4.** wonder

W	O	N	D	E	R	B	T
J	I	B	N	C	L	K	E
Y	L	V	O	Y	Z	B	
R	I	V	E	R	S	M	I
G	S	Q	R	R	Y	E	T
G	E	T	C	L	O	S	E

Visualization : 순서

주어진 단어를 이용해서 표를 완성하세요. 그리고 올바른 순서에 따라 1-4를 써 보세요.

- (왼쪽부터) trunks, bit / 4-1-3-2
- 1: "악어 아저씨는 점심식사로 무엇을 드실까?" 꼬마 코끼리는 궁금해했어요.
  2: "아저씨는 점심식사로 무엇을 드시나요?" 꼬마 코끼리가 물었어요.
  3: 악어 아저씨는 꼬마 코끼리의 코를 물고는 잡아당겼어요.
  4: 코끼리들은 긴 코를 갖게 되었어요.

Talk About It

- 코끼리들은 긴 코를 가지고 무슨 일을 할까요?
- 당신의 코와 코끼리의 코는 어떻게 다른가요?

Words to Know

듣고 따라 말해 보세요.

- breathe 숨쉬다
- touch 만지다
- dust 흙
- pick up 집어들다
- smell 냄새를 맡다
- spray 흩뿌리다
- body 몸
- protect 보호하다

Main Reading

코끼리들은 긴 코를 가지고 있어요.

그들은 코로 숨을 쉬고, 냄새를 맡고, 만지고, 먹고, 마신답니다.

이 코끼리는 물을 찾아 땅을 파기 위해 코를 사용할 수 있어요.

이 코끼리는 몸에 흙을 뿌리기 위해 코를 사용할 수 있어요.

이 코끼리는 물을 마시기 위해 코를 사용할 수 있어요.

이 코끼리는 땅콩을 줍기 위해 코를 사용할 수 있어요.

이 코끼리는 새끼를 만지기 위해 코를 사용할 수 있어요.

이 코끼리는 스스로를 보호하기 위해 코를 사용할 수 있어요.

코끼리들은 코로 많은 일들을 한답니다.

Key Expressions

A: 코끼리들은 코로 무슨 일을 할 수 있니?
B: 그들은 물을 찾아 땅을 팔 수 있어.

| 문제 정답 및 해설 |

Comprehension Check

읽고 알맞은 답을 고르세요.

1. 무엇에 관한 글인가요?   [정답 : a]

a. 코끼리들이 코로 무슨 일을 하는지에 관한 글이에요.

b. 코끼리들이 어떻게 물을 찾아 땅을 파는지에 관한 글이에요.

2. 코끼리들은 코로 무엇을 하나요?   [정답 : a]

a. 그들은 땅콩을 줍기 위해 코를 사용할 수 있어요.

b. 그들은 새끼를 들어올리기 위해 코를 사용할 수 있어요.

3. 코끼리들은 코로 숨쉬고, 냄새를 맡고, 만지고, 먹고, 마셔요.

    a. 물다   **b.** 숨쉬다   [정답 : b]

Sentence Focus

읽고 알맞은 문장을 고르세요.

1. ■ 그것은 물을 찾아 땅을 파기 위해서 코를 사용할 수 있어요.

□ 그것은 물을 뿌리기 위해서 코를 사용할 수 있어요.

2. ■ 그것은 새끼를 만지기 위해 코를 사용할 수 있어요.

□ 그것은 새끼에게 먹이를 주기 위해 코를 사용할 수 있어요.

3. ■ 그것은 물을 마시기 위해 코를 사용할 수 있어요.

□ 그것은 스스로를 보호하기 위해 코를 사용할 수 있어요.

Word Practice

그림에 알맞은 단어를 찾아 동그라미 하고 써 보세요.

1. pick up   **2.** smell   **3.** touch   **4.** protect

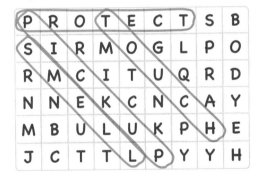

Visualization : 주제와 세부사항

주어진 단어를 이용해서 표를 완성하세요.

- (순서대로) dust / breathe
- 주제 – 코끼리들은 그들의 코를 가지고 많은 일들을 해요.
- 세부사항 – 코끼리들은 그들의 코로 물을 마실 수 있어요.
  - 코끼리들은 그들의 코로 흙을 뿌릴 수 있어요.
  - 코끼리들은 그들의 코로 숨을 쉴 수 있어요.
  - 코끼리들은 그들의 코로 먹을 수 있어요.

Talk About It

- 괴물은 어디에 사나요?
- 당신은 괴물을 무서워하나요?

Words to Know

듣고 따라 말해 보세요.

- afraid 두려워하는
- gym 체육관
- girl's room 여자 화장실
- locker 사물함

- library 도서관
- tiptoe 발끝으로 살금살금 걷다
- boy's room 남자 화장실
- shut 닫다

Main Reading

우리는 괴물을 찾으러 가는 중이에요.
우리는 두렵지 않아요!
괴물이 도서관에 있을까요?
아니면 체육관에 있을까요?
살금살금, 살금살금.
우리는 괴물을 찾으러 가는 중이에요.
우리는 두렵지 않아요!
괴물이 여자 화장실에 있을까요?
아니면 남자 화장실에 있을까요?
살금살금, 살금살금.
으악! 사물함 안에 괴물이 있어요!
다시 남자 화장실로, 여자 화장실로 돌아가요!
다시 체육관으로, 도서관으로 돌아가요!
쾅! 쾅! 쾅! 쾅!   문을 닫아요! 꽝!
우리는 두 번 다시 괴물을 찾으러 가지 않을 거예요!

Key Expressions

A: 괴물은 도서관에 있니?   B: 아니.

| 문제 정답 및 해설 |

Comprehension Check

읽고 알맞은 답을 고르세요.

1. 우리는 무엇을 하고 있나요?   [정답 : b]
   a. 우리는 학교에 가고 있어요.

b. 우리는 괴물을 찾으러 가고 있어요.

2. 우리는 어디에서 괴물을 발견하나요?   [정답 : b]
   a. 도서관에서   **b.** 사물함 안에서

3. 우리는 다시 괴물을 찾으러 가는 것이 두려워요.   [정답 : a]
   a. 두려운   **b.** 두렵지 않은

Sentence Focus

읽고 알맞은 문장을 고르세요.

1. ☐ 괴물이 여자 화장실에 있나요?
   ■ 괴물이 남자 화장실에 있나요?

2. ■ 사물함 안에 괴물이 있어요!
   ☐ 체육관에 괴물이 있어요!

3. ☐ 우리는 다시 체육관으로 돌아가요.
   ■ 우리는 다시 도서관으로 돌아가요.

Word Practice

그림에 알맞은 단어를 찾아 동그라미 하고 써 보세요.

1. afraid   **2.** tiptoe   **3.** shut   **4.** girl's room

G	I	R	L	'	S	R	O	O	M	T
Z	M	U	Y	L	D	H	B	S	O	I
S	I	G	D	V	O	O	U	I	U	P
H	E	W	P	E	J	U	N	T	A	T
H	A	F	R	A	I	D	A	Y	U	O
R	F	B	L	E	V	M	T	P	J	E
E	B	E	D	K	H	A	J	F	C	N

Visualization : 순서

주어진 단어를 이용해서 표를 완성하세요. 그리고 이야기 속에서 아이들이 방문한 장소들을 올바른 순서에 따라 1-5를 써 보세요.

- (순서대로) library, gym / 1-4-3-2-5
- 1: 도서관   2: 체육관   3: 여자 화장실
  4: 남자 화장실   5: 사물함

Talk About It

- 당신은 현장 학습을 가 본 적이 있나요?
- 어디로 갔었나요?

Words to Know

듣고 따라 말해 보세요.

- field trip 현장 학습
- kid 아이
- tank 수조
- dangerous 위험한
- aquarium 수족관
- starfish 불가사리
- shark 상어
- kill 죽이다, 해치다

Main Reading

2023년 4월 8일

일기장에게

오늘 우리 반은 현장 학습을 갔어.

우리는 수족관에 갔지.

우리 반의 모든 아이들이 현장 학습에 참여했어.

수족관에서 우리는 수조 안에 있는 불가사리들을 봤어.

우리는 우리 머리 위를 헤엄치는 상어들을 봤지.

우리는 상자해파리들도 봤어.

나는 상자해파리들이 매우 위험하다는 것을 배웠어.

그것들은 작은 아이 한 명을 3분 안에 해칠 수도 있어!

우리는 즐거운 하루를 보냈어!

우리가 올해 갔던 것 중 최고의 현장 학습이었어.

Key Expressions

A: 너는 수족관에서 무엇을 봤니?

B: 상자해파리들을 봤어.

문제 정답 및 해설 |

Comprehension Check

읽고 알맞은 답을 고르세요.

- 우리 반은 오늘 어디에 갔나요?   [정답 : a]
  a. 우리 반은 수족관으로 현장 학습을 갔어요.

  b. 우리 반은 바다로 현장 학습을 갔어요.

2. 우리는 수족관에서 무엇을 봤나요?   [정답 : a]
   a. 우리는 우리 머리 위를 헤엄치는 상어들을 봤어요.

   b. 우리는 불가사리들이 아이 한 명을 해치는 것을 봤어요.

3. 상자해파리들은 아이 한 명을 해칠 수도 있기 때문에 위험해요.
   a. 위험한   **b.** 친근한   [정답 : a]

Sentence Focus

읽고 알맞은 문장을 고르세요.

1. ■ 우리 반은 현장 학습을 갔어요.
   □ 우리 반은 낚시하러 갔어요.

2. ■ 우리 반의 모든 아이들이 현장 학습에 왔어요.
   □ 우리 반의 어떤 아이들도 현장 학습에 오지 않았어요.

3. ■ 우리는 수조 안에 있는 불가사리들을 봤어요.
   □ 우리는 수조 안에 있는 상어들을 봤어요.

Word Practice

그림에 알맞은 단어를 찾아 동그라미 하고 써 보세요.

1. field trip   **2.** kid   **3.** dangerous   **4.** kill

```
D A N G E R O U S
F I E L D T R I P
M Y T T B P K G M
Q K I L L Q D I J
Z D I O G D X J D
```

Visualization : 배경

주어진 단어를 이용해서 표를 완성하세요.

- (순서대로) aquarium / tank / sharks
- 어디서? – 수족관에서
- 무엇을? – 우리는 수조 안에 있는 불가사리들을 봤어요.
  - 우리는 우리 머리 위를 헤엄치는 상어들을 봤어요.
  - 우리는 위험한 상자해파리들을 봤어요.

Talk About It

- 친구가 당신을 밀치면 기분이 어떤가요?
- 그 친구에게 어떤 말을 할 수 있을까요?

Words to Know

듣고 따라 말해 보세요.

- shoulder 어깨
- class photo 학급 사진
- hurt 아프게 하다
- bully (약자를) 괴롭히는 사람
- face 얼굴
- message 문자 메시지
- laugh 웃다
- nice 좋은

Main Reading

프랜시스가 내 어깨를 밀쳤어요.
"그러지 마." 하고 내가 말했어요.
제시는 학급 사진 속 내 얼굴에 커다란 코를 그렸어요.
"그러지 마." 하고 내가 말했어요.
스티비는 일주일 동안 똑같은 문자 메시지를 나에게 보냈어요.
"아무도 너를 좋아하지 않아!"
"그러지 마." 하고 내가 말했어요.
나는 체육관에서 넘어져서 다쳤어요.
다른 아이들은 나를 보며 웃었어요.
"제발 그만해! 더이상 괴롭히지 마! 그건 나를 굉장히 아프게 해.
그건 좋은 일이 아니야!" 나는 외쳤어요.

Key Expressions

A: 내 어깨를 밀지 마.   B: 미안해.

| 문제 정답 및 해설 |

Comprehension Check

읽고 알맞은 답을 고르세요.

1. 무엇에 관한 글인가요?   [정답 : a]
   a. 학교 내 괴롭힘에 관한 글이에요.
   b. 학급 사진에 관한 글이에요.

2. 학교 내 괴롭힘에 대해 당신은 어떤 말을 할 수 있나요?

   a. 그것은 지루해요.   [정답 : b]
   b. 그것은 누군가를 아프게 할 수도 있어요.

3. 누군가 나를 괴롭힐 때 "하지 마."라고 말해야 해요.   [정답 : a]
   a. "하지 마."   **b.** "미안해."

Sentence Focus

읽고 알맞은 문장을 고르세요.

1. ■ 그가 내 어깨를 밀쳤어요.
   □ 그가 내 얼굴을 때렸어요.

2. ■ 그가 나를 비웃었어요.
   □ 그가 나에게 문자 메시지를 보냈어요.

3. ■ "더이상 괴롭히지 마!" 내가 외쳤어요.
   □ "멋지다!" 내가 외쳤어요.

Word Practice

그림에 알맞은 단어를 찾아 동그라미 하고 써 보세요.

1. shoulder   2. face   3. laugh   4. nice

Visualization : 원인과 결과

주어진 단어를 이용해서 표를 완성하세요.

- (왼쪽부터) message / hurts
- 왜인가요?
  - 프랜시스가 내 어깨를 밀쳤어요.
  - 제시가 학급 사진 속 내 얼굴에 커다란 코를 그렸어요.
  - 스티비가 일주일 동안 똑같은 나쁜 메시지를 나에게 보냈어요.
- 무슨 일이 일어났나요? – 그것은 나를 매우 아프게 해요.

Talk About It

- 당신은 소셜 미디어를 사용하나요?
- 당신은 소셜 미디어를 어떻게 사용하나요?

Words to Know

듣고 따라 말해 보세요.

- etiquette 에티켓, 예의
- comments 댓글
- post (웹사이트에) 올리다
- kind 친절한
- chat 채팅하다
- social media 소셜 미디어
- true 사실인
- tag 태그하다

Main Reading

당신은 소셜 미디어에서 채팅하는 것을 좋아하나요?

당신은 소셜 미디어에 댓글을 작성하는 것을 좋아하나요?

당신은 소셜 미디어에서 친구들을 태그하는 것을 좋아하나요?

소셜 미디어에 게시물을 올리기 전에 생각해 보세요.

당신의 메시지가 사실이 맞는지 생각해 보세요.

당신의 댓글이 친절한지 생각해 보세요.

당신의 친구들을 태그하는 것이 괜찮은지 생각해 보세요.

소셜 미디어는 위험할 수 있다는 것을 기억하세요.

당신의 친구들을 아프게 할 수 있어요.

악플러들은 사람들을 화나게 만들어요.

싫어요! 싫어요! 싫어요!

Key Expressions

A: 너는 소셜 미디어에서 무엇을 하는 것을 좋아하니?

B: 나는 사진을 올리는 것을 좋아해.

문제 정답 및 해설 |

Comprehension Check

읽고 알맞은 답을 고르세요.

무엇에 관한 글인가요?　　　　　　　　　　[정답 : a]

a. 소셜 미디어 에티켓이 왜 중요한지에 관한 글이에요.

b. 소셜 미디어에서 댓글을 작성하는 방법에 관한 글이에요.

2. 소셜 미디어에서 행동하기 전에 무엇을 해야 하나요?　[정답 : b]

a. 메시지가 재미있는지 생각해야 해요.

b. 메시지가 사실이 맞는지 생각해야 해요.

3. 소셜미디어는 위험할 수 있어요.　　　　　　[정답 : a]

a. 위험한　　　　b. 도움이 되는

Sentence Focus

읽고 알맞은 문장을 고르세요.

1. ■ 소셜 미디어에서 채팅하는 것을 좋아하나요?

　□ 당신의 친구들을 아프게 하는 것을 좋아하나요?

2. □ 그 메시지가 재미있는지 생각하세요.

　■ 그 메시지가 친절한지 생각하세요.

3. ■ 소셜 미디어는 누군가를 아프게할 수 있어요.

　□ 소셜 미디어는 누군가를 도울 수 있어요.

Word Practice

그림에 알맞은 단어를 찾아 동그라미 하고 써 보세요.

1. kind　**2.** post　**3.** chat　**4.** tag

L	U	F	R	E	W	O	P
L	P	D	D	C	T	A	G
B	O	N	H	K	I	N	D
G	S	A	K	R	N	D	L
S	T	D	P	J	R	R	X

Visualization : 원인과 결과

주어진 단어를 이용해서 표를 완성하세요.

- (왼쪽부터) true / Social media

왜인가요?	무슨 일이 일어났나요?
– 메시지가 사실이 아니에요. – 댓글이 친절하지 않아요. – 메시지가 도움이 되지 않아요.	⇨ 소셜 미디어는 누군가를 　아프게 할 수 있어요.

Talk About It

- 아이들은 무엇을 먹나요?
- 당신은 당신의 이가 어떤 모양인지 설명할 수 있나요?

Words to Know

듣고 따라 말해 보세요.

- tooth 이빨, 치아
- plant 식물
- large 큰
- chew 씹다
- flat 평평한, 고른
- sharp 날카로운
- front teeth 앞니
- fight 싸우다

Main Reading

오, 이럴수가! 정말 고른 이빨을 가지고 있군요!

내 고른 이빨은 내가 식물을 먹는 것을 도와줘요.

오, 이럴수가! 정말 날카로운 이빨을 가지고 있군요!

내 날카로운 이빨은 내가 동물을 먹는 것을 도와줘요.

오, 이럴수가! 정말 커다란 앞니를 가지고 있군요!

내 커다란 앞니는 내가 나뭇가지를 씹는 것을 도와줘요.

오, 이럴수가! 정말 거대한 이빨을 가지고 있군요!

내 거대한 이빨은 내가 싸우는 것을 도와줘요.

나는 고르고 뽀족한 이를 가지고 있어요.

내가 무엇을 먹는다고 생각하나요?

- 말　• 호랑이　• 비버　• 하마

Key Expressions

A: 정말 고른 이빨을 가지고 있구나!

B: 내 고른 이빨은 내가 식물을 먹는 것을 도와줘.

| 문제 정답 및 해설 |

Comprehension Check

읽고 알맞은 답을 고르세요.

1. 무엇에 관한 글인가요?　　　　　　　[정답 : b]

　　a. 동물들의 먹이에 관한 글이에요.

　　b. 동물들의 이빨에 관한 글이에요.

2. 동물들은 그들의 이빨을 어떻게 사용하나요?　[정답 : a]

　　a. 어떤 동물들은 이빨을 이용해서 먹이를 먹어요.

　　b. 어떤 동물들은 이빨을 이용해서 잡아요.

3. 말의 고른 이빨은 그것이 식물을 먹는 것을 도와줘요. [정답 : b]

　　a. 나뭇가지　　　**b.** 식물

Sentence Focus

읽고 알맞은 문장을 고르세요.

1. ☐ 정말 고른 이빨을 가지고 있군요!

　　■ 정말 날카로운 이빨을 가지고 있군요!

2. ☐ 나는 작은 이빨을 가지고 있어요.

　　■ 나는 거대한 이빨을 가지고 있어요.

3. ■ 내 이빨은 내가 나뭇가지 씹는 것을 도와줘요.

　　☐ 내 이빨은 내가 싸우는 것을 도와줘요.

Word Practice

그림에 알맞은 단어를 찾아 동그라미 하고 써 보세요.

1. tooth　**2.** flat　**3.** plant　**4.** fight

Visualization : 분류하기

주어진 단어를 이용해서 표를 완성하세요.

- (왼쪽부터) chew / Sharp
- 동물의 이빨
- 고른 이빨: 식물을 먹어요, 말
- 날카로운 이빨: 동물을 먹어요, 호랑이
- 커다란 앞니: 나뭇가지를 씹어요, 비버
- 거대한 이빨: 싸워요, 하마

Talk About It

- 어떤 동물이 알에서 태어나나요?
- 어린 동물이 어떻게 알의 껍데기를 깨고 나올까요?

Words to Know

듣고 따라 말해 보세요.

- lay an egg 알을 낳다
- young animal 새끼 동물
- egg tooth 난치
- eggshell 알껍데기
- color 색깔
- grow 자라다
- break 깨다
- hatch 부화하다

Main Reading

어떤 동물은 알을 낳아요.

어떤 동물은 한 번에 단 하나의 알을 낳아요.

다른 동물은 한 번에 많은 알을 낳죠.

알의 모양은 다양해요.

알의 크기도 다양하죠.

알의 색깔도 다양해요.

새끼 동물은 알 속에서 안전하게 자라요.

새끼 동물은 난치를 가지고 있어요.

난치는 새끼 동물이 알껍데기를 깨는 것을 도와줘요.

난치는 새끼 동물이 부화한 후에 떨어져 나가요.

Key Expressions

A: 너는 알에 대해서 무엇을 알고 있니?

B: 알은 크기가 다양해.

문제 정답 및 해설 |

Comprehension Check

고 알맞은 답을 고르세요.

무엇에 관한 글인가요?   [정답 : b]

a. 새끼 동물의 이빨에 관한 글이에요.

b. 동물의 알에 관한 글이에요.

무엇이 새끼 동물이 알껍데기를 깨는 것을 도와주나요?

a. 난치   [정답 : a]

b. 다 자란 동물들

3. 새끼 동물이 <u>부화한</u> 후에, 난치는 떨어져 나가요.   [정답 : a]

a. 부화하다   b. 자라다

Sentence Focus

읽고 알맞은 문장을 고르세요.

1. ☐ 어떤 동물은 한 번에 단 하나의 알을 낳아요.
   ■ 어떤 동물은 한 번에 많은 알을 낳아요.

2. ■ 알은 색깔이 다양해요.
   ☐ 알은 모양이 다양해요.

3. ☐ 새끼 동물은 알 속에서 안전하게 자라요.
   ■ 새끼 동물은 알껍데기를 깨고 나와요.

Word Practice

그림에 알맞은 단어를 찾아 동그라미 하고 써 보세요.

1. color   2. grow   3. break   4. hatch

H	G	W	N	V	M	W	C
A	V	G	Y	N	O	Y	O
T	B	R	E	A	K	T	L
C	X	R	G	R	O	W	O
H	T	Y	B	T	A	Y	R
M	L	W	R	B	K	M	A

Visualization : 주제와 세부사항

주어진 단어를 이용해서 표를 완성하세요.

- (순서대로) <u>colors</u> / <u>egg tooth</u>
- 주제 – 어떤 동물은 알을 낳아요.
- 세부사항 – 한 번에 하나의 알 / 한 번에 많은 알
  - 다양한 모양 / 다양한 크기 / 다양한 <u>색깔</u>
  - 알 속에서 안전하게 자라요. /
    <u>난치</u>를 가지고 있어요.

Talk About It

- 당신은 얼마나 자주 밤에 밖에서 걷나요?
- 무엇이 보이나요?

Words to Know

듣고 따라 말해 보세요.

- window 창문
- miss 그리워하다
- street 거리
- glow 빛나다
- moon 달
- night 밤
- dark 어두운
- arrive 도착하다

Main Reading

나는 창밖을 바라봐요.

달이 보여요.

마치 할머니의 얼굴처럼 보여요.

"아빠, 할머니가 보고 싶어요. 지금 가서 뵈어도 돼요?" 내가 말해요.

아빠와 나는 밤에 밖에서 걸어요.

할머니는 그 길의 건너편에 살고 계세요.

밖은 어두워요.

어둠 속에서는 물체를 보는 것이 어려워요.

하지만 어둠 속에서 빛을 찾기는 쉬워요.

"보세요! 별들이 오늘은 더 밝게 빛나요." 나는 외쳐요.

우리는 걷다가 어둠 속에서 무엇인가 빛나는 것을 봐요.

"야옹!"

할머니의 고양이인 키티네요.

우리는 벌써 할머니 댁에 도착했어요.

Key Expressions

A: 너는 밤하늘에서 무엇이 보이니?

B: 나는 밤하늘의 별들이 보여.

| 문제 정답 및 해설 |

Comprehension Check

읽고 알맞은 답을 고르세요.

1. 나는 창밖에서 무엇을 보나요? [정답 : b]

　　a. 할머니의 얼굴을 봐요.　　**b.** 달을 봐요.

2. 아빠와 나는 어디에 가나요? [정답 : a]

　　a. 할머니를 뵈러　　　**b.** 키티를 찾으러

3. 어둠 속에서 빛을 찾는 것은 쉬워요. [정답 : b]

　　a. 할머니의 집　　　**b.** 빛

Sentence Focus

읽고 알맞은 문장을 고르세요.

1. □ 나는 할머니의 고양이를 봐요.

　　■ 나는 달을 봐요.

2. ■ 우리는 할머니 댁에 도착했어요.

　　□ 우리는 할머니 댁으로 걸어나갔어요.

3. ■ 우리는 어둠 속에서 무엇인가 빛나는 것을 봐요.

　　□ 우리는 어둠 속에서 무엇인가 나는 것을 봐요.

Word Practice

그림에 알맞은 단어를 찾아 동그라미 하고 써 보세요.

1. window　**2.** night　**3.** street　**4.** arrive

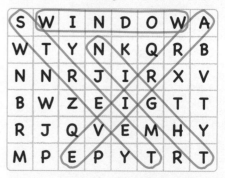

Visualization : 원인과 결과

주어진 단어를 이용해서 표를 완성하세요.

- (순서대로) miss / dark

왜인가요?	무슨 일이 일어났나요?
– 나는 할머니가 보고 싶어요.	⇨ 아빠와 나는 할머니를 뵈러 가요.
– 어둠 속에서 빛을 찾는 것은 쉬워요.	⇨ 우리는 어둠 속에서 빛나는 키티의 눈을 봐요.

Talk About It

- 당신은 별을 보는 것을 좋아하나요?
- 당신은 언제 별을 볼 수 있나요?

Words to Know

듣고 따라 말해 보세요.

- jar 단지, 병
- tinfoil 은박지
- roll 둥글게 감다
- paper clip 종이 클립
- poke 찌르다
- wrap 싸다
- turn on 켜다
- turn off 끄다

Main Reading

〈준비물: 단지, 은박지, 가위, 종이 클립, 테이프, 스마트폰〉
별 단지를 만들어요.

〈은박지 치수를 재요.〉

1. 단지를 꺼내서 은박지로 둥글게 감으세요.
2. 은박지를 자르세요.

〈별을 만들어요.〉

3. 종이 클립을 사용해서 은박지에 구멍을 뚫으세요.
4. 원하는 만큼 많은 구멍을 뚫으세요.

〈별 단지〉

5. 은박지로 단지를 감싸세요.
6. 은박지를 테이프로 확실히 고정시키세요.

〈별을 감상해요.〉

7. 스마트폰 불빛을 켜세요.
8. 스마트폰을 단지 안에 넣으세요.
9. 방의 조명을 끄세요.

Key Expressions

A: 별 단지는 어떻게 만들지?   B: 은박지를 잘라.

문제 정답 및 해설 |

Comprehension Check

듣고 알맞은 답을 고르세요.

. 무엇에 관한 글인가요?   [정답 : a]
    a. 별 단지를 만드는 방법에 관한 글이에요.
    b. 밤에 별을 보는 것에 관한 글이에요.

2. 단지에 어떻게 별을 만들 수 있나요?   [정답 : a]
    a. 은박지에 구멍을 뚫어서
    b. 단지에 별을 그려서

3. 별을 즐기기 위해서 조명을 <u>꺼야</u> 해요.   [정답 : b]
    a. 켜다   b. 끄다

Sentence Focus

읽고 알맞은 문장을 고르세요.

1. ■ 은박지를 자르세요.
    □ 종이 클립을 자르세요.

2. □ 단지를 은박지로 둥글게 감으세요.
    ■ 은박지에 구멍을 뚫으세요.

3. □ 스마트폰 불빛을 켜세요.
    ■ 은박지로 단지를 감싸세요.

Word Practice

그림에 알맞은 단어를 찾아 동그라미 하고 써 보세요.

1. jar   **2.** roll   **3.** poke   **4.** wrap

L	K	J	R	Z	W	H	P
D	K	O	J	R	J	O	O
Z	L	M	A	A	D	L	K
L	P	P	L	Z	J	E	E
T	U	R	N	A	D	S	Z
O	F	F	R	O	N	P	Q

Visualization : 순서

주어진 단어를 이용해서 표를 완성하세요. 그리고 별 단지 만드는
올바른 순서에 따라 1-4를 써 보세요.

· (순서대로) <u>Turn on</u>, <u>Poke</u> / <u>3</u>-<u>1</u>-<u>4</u>-<u>2</u>
· 1: 은박지에 구멍을 <u>뚫어요</u>.   2: 은박지로 단지를 감싸요.
  3: 스마트폰 불빛을 <u>켜요</u>.   4: 방의 조명을 꺼요.

Talk About It

- 당신은 초콜릿을 좋아하나요?
- 당신은 초콜릿이 어떻게 만들어지는지 알고 있나요?

Words to Know

듣고 따라 말해 보세요.

- cocoa 코코아
- harvest 수확, 수확하다
- bean 콩
- sack 자루
- farm 농장
- remove 제거하다
- carry 운반하다
- dream 꿈

Main Reading

내 이름은 압둘이에요.

나는 열 살이죠.

나는 코코아 농장에서 일해요.

지금은 농장의 수확철이에요.

나는 아침 일찍 일어나요.

먼저, 나는 코코아 꼬투리를 수확해요.

그런 다음, 꼬투리를 열고 콩을 빼내죠.

그 후에는 콩 자루를 트럭으로 옮겨요.

나는 하루 종일 일해요.

더위 속에서 일하는 것은 몹시 힘들답니다.

나는 꿈이 있어요.

언젠가 나는 학교에 가고 싶어요.

Key Expressions

A: 너는 코코아 농장에서 무엇을 하니?

B: 나는 코코아 꼬투리를 수확해.

| 문제 정답 및 해설 |

Comprehension Check

읽고 알맞은 답을 고르세요.

1. 무엇에 관한 이야기인가요?   [정답 : a]
   a. 압둘이라는 소년에 관한 이야기예요.
   b. 코코아 농장에 관한 이야기예요.

2. 압둘은 코코아 농장에서 무슨 일을 하나요?   [정답 : a]
   a. 그는 코코아 꼬투리를 수확해요.
   b. 그는 트럭을 운전해요.

3. 압둘은 언젠가 학교에 가는 것을 <u>꿈꿔요</u>.   [정답 : b]
   a. 일해요   b. 꿈꿔요

Sentence Focus

읽고 알맞은 문장을 고르세요.

1. ■ 나는 코코아 꼬투리를 수확해요.
   □ 나는 코코아 꼬투리를 열어요.

2. ■ 나는 꼬투리에서 콩을 빼내요.
   □ 나는 자루에서 코코아 꼬투리를 빼내요.

3. □ 나는 트럭을 옮겨요.
   ■ 나는 콩 자루를 옮겨요.

Word Practice

그림에 알맞은 단어를 찾아 동그라미 하고 써 보세요.

1. carry   2. remove   3. harvest   4. bean

R	D	M	Y	R	B	T	T
C	E	P	J	L	Z	A	J
J	A	M	M	B	E	A	N
K	J	R	O	V	A	P	X
B	Y	N	R	V	N	E	M
L	J	A	D	Y	E	D	B
G	H	A	R	V	E	S	T

Visualization : 결론 내리기

주어진 단어를 이용해서 표를 완성하세요.

- (순서대로) <u>farm</u> / <u>school</u>
- 압둘은 열 살이에요. / 코코아 <u>농장</u>에서 일하는 것은 매우 힘들어요. / 압둘은 학교에 가고 싶어 해요.
  ⇨ 결론: 압둘은 다른 아이들처럼 <u>학교</u>에 다녀야 해요.

Talk About It

- 사진 속의 아이들은 무엇을 하고 있나요?
- 당신은 어떤 어린이들이 왜 일을 한다고 생각하나요?

Words to Know

듣고 따라 말해 보세요.

- children 아이들
- cotton 목화
- sell 팔다
- brick 벽돌
- work 일하다
- all day long 하루 종일
- sweet 단 것 (사탕 및 초콜릿류)
- harsh 가혹한

Main Reading

많은 아이들이 일을 해요.
그들은 그들의 가족을 돕기 위해 일하죠.
일을 할 때, 그들은 다른 것을 할 시간이 없어요.
로지타는 학교에 가길 원해요.
하지만 그녀는 하루 종일 목화를 따야 하죠.
페드로는 축구를 하길 원해요.
하지만 그는 온종일 단 것을 팔아야 하죠.
다이애나는 글 읽는 법을 배우길 원해요.
하지만 그녀는 하루 종일 벽돌을 만들어야 해요.
아이들이 일하는 것은 너무 가혹해요.
모든 아이들은 아이인 것을 즐길 시간이 필요해요.

Key Expressions

A: 어떤 아이들은 가족을 돕기 위해 무엇을 하니?
B: 그들은 온종일 목화를 따.

| 문제 정답 및 해설 |

Comprehension Check

읽고 알맞은 답을 고르세요.

1. 무엇에 관한 글인가요?　　　　　　　　　　[정답 : b]
  a. 세계 각지의 직업에 관한 글이에요.
  b. 일하는 아이들에 관한 글이에요.

2. 왜 아이들이 일을 하나요?　　　　　　　　　[정답 : b]
  a. 학교에 가기 위해 일해요.
  b. 가족을 돕기 위해 일해요.

3. 아이들이 하루 종일 일하는 것은 너무 가혹해요.　[정답 : a]
  a. 가혹한　　　　**b.** 달콤한

Sentence Focus

읽고 알맞은 문장을 고르세요.

1. ■ 그녀는 온종일 목화를 따야만 해요.
　　□ 그녀는 온종일 벽돌을 만들어야만 해요.

2. ■ 그는 축구하기를 원해요.
　　□ 그는 글 읽는 법을 배우길 원해요.

3. □ 그들은 일할 시간이 필요해요.
　　■ 그들은 아이인 것을 즐길 시간이 필요해요.

Word Practice

그림에 알맞은 단어를 찾아 동그라미 하고 써 보세요.

1. sell　**2.** work　**3.** sweet　**4.** harsh

A	L	S	E	L	L	L	O	W
S	R	H	D	D	Q	D	N	O
D	W	N	A	B	Q	E	B	R
X	N	E	K	R	R	T	P	K
M	Q	P	E	D	S	M	Q	J
T	B	D	L	T	G	H	K	M

Visualization : 저자의 의도

주어진 단어를 이용해서 표를 완성하세요.

- (순서대로) cotton / work
- 로지타는 온종일 목화를 따야 해요. / 페드로는 온종일 단 것을 팔아야 해요. / 다이애나는 온종일 벽돌을 만들어야 해요.
  ⇨ 저자의 의도: 아이들이 일하는 것은 너무 가혹해요.
　　모든 아이들은 아이인 것을 즐길 시간이 필요해요.

미국교과서 READING Level 2 권별 교과 목록

1권 2.1

1. Social Studies
2. Language Arts
3. Health & Wellness
4. Language Arts
5. Health & Wellness
6. Social Studies
7. Social Studies
8. Health & Wellness
9. Social Studies
10. Science
11. Science
12. Math
13. Social Studies
14. Science
15. Social Studies
16. Math
17. Science
18. Science
19. Ethics
20. Science

2권 2.2

1. Health & Wellness
2. Science
3. Language Arts
4. Social Studies
5. Language Arts
6. Health & Wellness
7. Language Arts
8. Social Studies
9. Language Arts
10. Science
11. Language Arts
12. Language Arts
13. Ethics
14. Ethics
15. Language Arts
16. Science
17. Language Arts
18. Art & Crafts
19. Language Arts
20. Ethics

3권 2.3

1. Social Studies
2. Art & Crafts
3. Health & Wellness
4. Social Studies
5. Language Arts
6. Social Studies
7. Ethics
8. Social Studies
9. Language Arts
10. Science
11. Language Arts
12. Science
13. Social Studies
14. Science
15. Science
16. Science
17. Social Studies
18. Social Studies
19. Language Arts
20. Science

길벗스쿨 공식 카페, <기적의 공부방>에서 함께 공부해요!

기적의 학습단

홈스쿨링 응원 프로젝트! 학습단에 참여하여 공부 습관도 기르고 칭찬 선물도 받으세요!

도서 서평단

길벗스쿨의 책을 가장 먼저 체험하고, 기획에도 직접 참여해 보세요.

알찬 학습 팁

엄마표 학습 노하우를 나누며 우리 아이 맞춤 학습법을 함께 찾아요.

<기적의 공부방> https://cafe.naver.com/gilbutschool